THE SIBERIAN BOLIDE

TRANSLATED AND PUBLISHED IN ENGLISH WITH PERMISSION.
***
PAPERBACK ISBN: 979-8-9902858-1-1
EPUB ISBN: 979-8-2248070-2-4
***
WRITTEN BY ROBERT KONSTANTY LEŚNIAKIEWICZ
PUBLISHED BY ROYAL HAWAIIAN PRESS
COVER ART BY TYRONE ROSHANTHA
TRANSLATED BY RAFAL STACHOWSKY
PUBLISHING ASSISTANCE: DOROTA RESZKE
***
VERSION NUMBER 1.00

THE SIBERIAN BOLIDE

ANTHOLOGY

BY ROBERT LEŚNIAKIEWICZ

Table of Contents

PART I
A. I. Wojciechowskij -
WHAT WAS IT? – THE MYSTERY OF PODKAMIENNAYA TUNGUSKA

0. FROM THE TRANSLATOR

I had long been trying to prepare a translation of A.I. Wojciechowski's work since I first had the opportunity to encounter it in 1992, thanks to my Colleague, an ufologist from Russia with Polish origins, M.A. Władysław Bielecki from Orenburg, who sent it to me as part of his cooperation with the Orenburskom Ufołogiczieski Kłubom.

The reason I was thinking about it is that it is not easy to write something new and to speak on an issue that, like the mythical Atlantis, has not left the pages of the exo- and esoteric press since 1908.

Who is the Author? Dr. A.I. Wojciechowskij[1] is a member of the Russian Federation (formerly USSR) Cosmonautics

---

[1] In the original, "candidate of technical sciences". In the former USSR and today's Russia there is a separate system of degrees and titles, which in the following parts of the texts I bring to the system in force in Poland and Europe. The title of the original Russian is "Czto eto było? - Tajna Podkamiennoj Tunguski," Moscow 1991, translated by Robert K.

Federation Scientific and Technical Council Office, author of several books and brochures and papers in the trade press. The main topics covered by him are: scientific and technical achievements and prospects for the development of cosmonautics, the coexistence of human civilization with the Cosmos, the modern problems of Atlantisology.

For me, the fall of the Tunguska Meteorite, is also a family affair. Literally, because my grandfather on my mother's side - Franciszek Baranowicz - also found himself in the Podkamennaya Tunguska area during his travels in Siberia between 1905 and 1918, where, among other things, he fought the Japanese at Port Arthur and on the mounds of Manchuria. Although he was not at the very epicenter of the explosion, he spoke with eyewitnesses of the fall, which he himself had also witnessed, he saw the forest cavings, the burned and scorched trees, and he was one hundred percent convinced that it was not a meteorite fall, for he had also had the opportunity to see the fall of the Łowicz Meteorite and could compare the two events and accounts of them. They were two different things to him! When telling my sister Wiktoria and me about them, he always emphasized the differences between the two events...

Some may say that the topic has gotten old. Perhaps - but the issue of the Tunguska Bolide never gets old, because it is a press evergreen - a thing like a hunter's stew repeatedly warm-over and each time only gaining flavor, without losing its value by any means. Just such a press hunter's stew!... And this is how it will remain until we find a satisfactory explanation, and with our luck,

I know that even if such an explanation is found - there will always be someone who does not like it for one reason or another and will warm-over it again - just like hunter's stew!

I have tried to make as accurate as possible a translation of this work. I have included all my comments in footnotes and appendices, which I hope will deepen the Reader's knowledge of the subject. I hope you, the Reader, will be pleased with it. I wish you a pleasant reading experience.

Jordanów, June - October 1999

1. TO THE READER FROM THE AUTHOR

On the morning of June 30, 1908, an enormous bolide was observed shining brightly over Siberia and exploded with a powerful explosion after reaching the region of the Podkamennaya Tunguska River. The event went down in the history of meteoritics and astronomy, and it is considered a phenomenon of Nature.

Of course, mysteries are needed, especially those against which science has fall by the wayside - simply because people will always seek, discover the undiscovered, learn the unknowable what generations of soulless scientists have failed to know.

The path to the knowledge of scientific truth leads from the collection of facts, their systematization, generalization and rethinking. Facts, and only facts, become the foundation of a working hypothesis born during the researcher's busywork.

The author over the course of a quarter of a century collected materials on this issue, the Tunguska Meteorite problem, which were published in scientific works and monographs, popular science books, and finally in papers and articles, etc.

However, the huge amount of information collected by the Author poses a difficulty, because which of them must be selected to give the Reader in such a way that it is informative and not too boring? This was the number one question posed by the Author of this work.

Time brings more and more new versions and conjectures about the nature of the Tunguska Phenomenon, but somehow scholars cannot reach final conclusions, because this catastrophe by no means fits into the canons of classical meteorites. This cosmic body tore apart and disappeared entirely unlike that observed in the case of "proper" meteorites.

An astonishing matter, but the presence of so many hypotheses and explanations, versions and suggestions - and there are no comparative analyses, and no one has conducted a more detailed study as a basis for them. The following work is an attempt to make such an analysis.[2] This position has allowed him to formulate several closely standing hypotheses that may explain all or almost all the mysteries of the nature of the Tunguska explosion, including the mystery of the absence of any Tunguska body fragments.

The author does not pretend to present the whole issue of the Tunguska Meteorite, but hopes that this will allow the Reader to get closer to understanding the Tunguska Phenomenon.

---

[2] The Russian scientist P.I. Privalov, in an article titled "Hypotheses related to the fall of the Tunguska Meteorite" in "Kroki w nieznane" (Steps into the unknown), Warsaw 1971, makes such an analysis from the point of view of hypotheses formulated in 390 articles, 180 papers, 550 reports, 60 novels, 10 monographs and 5 movies. The total as of January 1, 1969 was as many as 80 in 8 categories. This analysis was posted by the monthly magazine "Priroda" No. 5/1969. From myself, I add three more hypotheses to this list in Part II of this study.

2. SOME CIRCUMSTANCES OF THE DISASTER

In the early morning of June 30, 1908, over the territory of the southern part of Central Siberia, many witnesses observed a fantastic spectacle: something huge and glowing was flying in the sky. According to the accounts of some, it was a glowing sphere, while others claimed that it was a fiery sheaf with spikes backwards, while a third saw in this phenomenon a burning log... Flying across the sky, the fiery body left a trail, like a normal meteorite. Its flight was also manifested by many sound phenomena, which were recorded by thousands of eyewitnesses within a radius of several hundred kilometers and caused fright and, in some places, panic.

Around 07:15 IRKT (local time)[3] the residents of the Vanavara factories, located on the banks of the Podkamennaya Tunguska River, a right tributary of the Yenisei, saw a blindingly bright sphere in the northern part of the sky that was brighter than the sun. The sphere transformed into a fiery column. After these luminous phenomena, witnesses felt the earth shake, then there was a powerful bang repeated many times, like lightning strikes in a thunderstorm.

The rumble and thunder shook everyone around, and it was heard within a radius of 1,200 kilometers from the epicenter of the disaster. Trees fell as if mowed down, window panes flew out of windows, while huge waves resembling water embankments appeared on rivers. Terrified animals rampaged around the taiga

---

[3] Precisely 07:17.11 IRKT that is 00:17 GMT or 01:17 Warsaw time (CEST).

in panic. Within a radius of more than a hundred kilometers from the center of the explosion, the ground trembled and window frames broke.

One witness was thrown backwards by the shock for 3 fathoms.[4] As it was later clarified, the shock wave knocked down trees in the taiga over an area with a radius of 30 kilometers. From the powerful impact of light and thermal radiation and a torrent of flared gases, a forest fire arose, and within a radius of tens of kilometers, vegetation cover was burned.

The sounds and echoes of the explosion-induced earthquake were recorded with seismographs in Irkutsk (Russia), Tashkent (Uzbekistan), Slutsk (Belarus) and Tbilisi (Georgia), as well as in Jena (Germany). The air shockwave caused by the incredible explosion circled the globe twice. Its presence was reported in Copenhagen (Denmark), Zagreb (Croatia), Washington DC, Potsdam (Germany), London and Jakarta (Indonesia), and several other places on the planet.

A few minutes after the explosion, a magnetic storm began, which lasted nearly four hours. This storm, as could be inferred from the descriptions, was remarkably similar to those currently observed in the Earth's atmo- and magnetosphere after test explosions of nuclear and thermonuclear "devices".

Strange phenomena were occurring all over the world within days of the mysterious explosion in the taiga. On the night of 30.VI./1.VII.1908, in more than 150 points of Western Siberia, Central Asia, the European part of Russia and in Europe, it was

---

[4] 1 fathom = 2,13 m.

practically no night, because in the sky, at an altitude of about 80 km, hung silvery clouds shining with strong light. As time passed, the intensity of these "white nights of 1908" decreased significantly, and already on July 4 this "cosmic fireworks" came to a complete end, nevertheless various luminous phenomena were observed in the Earth's atmosphere until the end of July 1908.[5]

Let's pay attention to one more fact that is related to the June 30, 1908 explosion. At a California actinometer station[6] a clear opacity of the atmosphere and a significant decrease in solar radiation were found. It was comparable to that found during strong volcanic eruptions. This is how some specific data about the Tunguska Explosion in 1908 looks like.

Anyway, that year - according to newspapers and magazines - abounded in a multitude of "celestial" as well as "terrestrial" unusual phenomena and natural phenomena. Thus, for example, in the spring of 1908, extremely devastating floods caused by heavy snowfall in Switzerland in late May were reported! - while a cloud of dense dust was observed over the Atlantic Ocean. The press of the time regularly reported on comets that were seen on Russian territory, several earthquakes, strange phenomena and extraordinary events that resulted from unknown causes.

Let's stop for a moment at one unusual optical phenomenon that was observed over Brest (Belarus), on February 22, 1908. In

---

[5] Silver clouds can be observed every summer in the mid-latitudes of the northern hemisphere. They consist of iron particles and suspend at an altitude of 80 km. Their origin has not been satisfactorily explained to this day!...

[6] Actinometry - the study of solar activity.

the morning, when the weather was clear and the air was transparent, a strongly luminous spot appeared on the northeastern side of the sky, above the horizon, rapidly approaching and taking the shape of the letter V. The object was moving from east to north. Its brightness initially very bright decreased, but the size increased. Within half an hour the visibility of the spot became very small, and after an hour and a half the object definitely disappeared. The length of its arms was enormous! Doesn't this information remind me of all the reports of UFO sightings that have been literally flooding us in recent times?[7] And all these most unexpected events and phenomena immediately preceded the catastrophe...

The aurora borealis was observed on the central Volga on the nights of 17/18 and 18/19.VI.

Since June 21, 1908, i.e. ten days before the catastrophe, the sky over Europe and Western Siberia was lit up in many places by bright and colorful auroras.

On the night of 23/24.VI over the area of Yurev[8] and some towns along the Baltic Sea, bright purple auroras appeared in the evening and at night, reminiscent of those observed a quarter of a century earlier, after the terrible - identified as cataclysmic - eruption and eventual explosion of the Krakatoa volcano.[9]

---

[7] No, it does not remind me of any UFO sighting, instead it reminds me of the passage of a cloud of space dust near the Earth without entering its atmosphere.

[8] Formerly Dorpat, today Tatru in Estonia.

[9] The eruption of the Krakatoa volcano (Rakata Crater) on August 23, 1883, ejected as much as 18 km3 of rock and tephra into the atmosphere, killing

White nights were no longer the monopoly of the North. Long silvery clouds glistened in the sky, stretched latitudinally - from east to west.[10] The number of such sightings has increased significantly since June 27. Frequent flights of bright meteors were reported. Tension was felt in nature, the approach of something unusual...

It should be noted that in the spring, summer and autumn of 1908, researchers found a significant increase in the level of activity of meteor swarms. The number of press reports on observations of meteor falls and meteorites from this period is many times greater than in other years. Bright bolides were seen in England, the European part of Russia, the Baltic republics, Central Asia, Siberia and China.

At the end of June 1908, an expedition of Geographical Society member A. Makarenko was working on Katonga - as locals call the Podobkamennaya Tunguska. I managed to find a short report on his work. It said that the expedition took measurements of Katonga's shores, its depths, fairways[11], etc. - but it doesn't mention some unusual events observed in connection with the meteorite fall and other phenomena accompanying the event... And this is one of the biggest mysteries of the Tunguska event! - well, because how could it have happened that Makarenko's expedition did not notice the luminous phenomenon flying over

---

about 36,000 people at the same time!

[10] "Today's" silvery clouds are more like lint or drapery glowing silvery against a dark sky background.

[11] Waterways.

the taiga, nor hear the monstrous bang with which the fall of the cosmic visitor into the forests of Siberia was manifested???[12]

For now, let's stay with this one of the earliest puzzles related to the Tunguska Explosion, as we will continue to come across facts of this nature more than once.

Unfortunately, to this day we do not have any testimony about whether there were scholars among the eyewitnesses who would take it upon themselves to verify its authenticity, let alone go to the site of the explosion and examine things in situ.

It is true that from the pre-revolutionary press, the memories of local residents and some St. Petersburg scholars, information has come to us that in 1909-1910 some people risked their lives to go to the site of the Tunguska Explosion and saw unusual things and phenomena there. Who were they? Who organized this expedition of theirs... There are no official reports about it, and traces of this mysterious expedition remain unknown...[13]

The first expedition, of which there are reliable records, was organized in 1911 by the Omsk Land and Water Road Authority. It was headed by engineer Vyacheşlav Shishkov, who later became a prominent writer. The expedition passed a great distance from

---

[12] Against all appearances, this is not as strange as the Author suggests, because in Jerzmanowice, near Kraków, there was an almost identical incident on January 14, 1993, and if it were not for the media, no one except the locals would have known about it... I will talk more about the Jerzmanowice Unusual Thing in Part II of this study.

[13] According to the Conspiracy Theory of History, they were most likely Freemasons who went there to cover the traces of the event and create the legend of the landing of the Visitors from Space - sic!

the epicenter of the explosion, although it discovered a huge forest howl in the Nizhna Tunguska region, which, however, was not linked to the meteorite fall...

And finally, a few words on terminology, names and abreviation. Publications about the unusual phenomenon more or less objective, and even with elements of disinformation (???) appeared in Siberian newspapers: "Sibirskaya zhyezhn," "Sibir," "Golos Tomsk," and "Krasnoyarsk" in the period from June to July 1908. In these, as well as in the riveting calendar published by O. Kirchnier (Sankt Petersburg) for 1910, the meteorite was called Filimonovsky, not Tungusky. The name "Tunguska Meteorite" appeared and became a permanent part of scientific terminology only in 1927.

The name Tunguska Meteorite should not mislead anyone, although, as the famous researcher of this phenomenon V. Bronstein said, we have fallen into a terminological trap here: after all, meteorites are called cosmic bodies that fall to Earth. However, recently in scientific and popular literature, authors use the term "meteorite" - and this is due to the effects of its fall. Today we no longer hear the objection that the "Tunguska Body" cannot be put in a row with iron or stone meteorites, which usually fall to Earth.[14]

The point is that giant meteorites with a mass of thousands of tons - and the mass of the Tunguska Meteorite was estimated to be at least 100,000 tons - should pierce the Earth's atmosphere and penetrate its surface, forming craters.[15] In our case, there should

---

[14] We divide meteorites into: chondrites and achondrites, amphoterites, carbonaceous chondrites, pallazites, mesosiderites, ataxites, hexadrites, octahedrons, enstatite and olivine chondrites.

be a crater with a diameter of at least 1.5 km and a depth of several hundred meters. Nothing of this kind occurred!...

There was and is no Tunguska meteorite! - Such a conclusion was reached by researchers in the early 1980s. Paradox? No. It was simply a clarification of terminology. A more accurate and appropriate term emerged: "Tunguska Cosmic Body"... - I, however, will keep the usual form: Tunguska Meteorite and in this work, I introduce the following abbreviations: TM - Tunguska Meteorite; TCB - Tunguska Cosmic Body and TP - Tunguska Phenomenon.

2.1. Kulik's expeditions

The legal discoverer of TM is Leonid Alekseevich Kulik (1883-1942), to whom science owes the fact that this phenomenon has not gone into oblivion.

Scientific research of the Tunguska problem began with a trifle. In 1921, L. Kulik, a 38-year-old geophysicist, tore a page from his calendar. At the time, he was a researcher with V.I. Vernadsky at the Museum of Mineralogy of the Academy of Sciences of the Soviet Union, when he read from the calendar sheet about a meteorite fall in 1908. This is how the scientist, who deals with "stones from the sky" on a daily basis, learned about

---

[15] Such craters are called impact craters. In Poland we have several post-impact formations: Morasko near Poznań, Frombork and the Złotoryja-Jaworsk Formation in Lower Silesia.

observations in the Yenisei Governorate of the flight of a huge bolide, and immediately wanted to find the place of its fall, and make the meteorite itself a scientific success.

In 1921-1922, Kulik undertook a reconnaissance expedition to Eastern Siberia. During this outing, he collected a large number of eyewitness testimonies about the event, which had taken place in the taiga 13 years earlier, and on the basis of these he made the first description of the disaster area and compiled the course of events. Let's note the following important circumstance: well, Kulik believed that the cause of the 1908 catastrophe could have been the collision of the Earth with a comet (!!!) - however, with persistence from the beginning to the end of his research, he searched for fragments of a giant meteorite, which broke into several parts in flight.

In the summer of 1924, geologist S. V. Obruchev - a member-correspondent of the AN of the USSR and a well-known author of SF novels - while studying the geology and geomorphology of the Tunguska Coal Basin, questioned locals about the circumstances surrounding the fall of the "heavenly visitor" at Kulik's request while in Vanavara. Obruchev managed to find out about the huge forest uprooting 100 kilometers north of Vanavar, but was unable to reach them.

Nineteen years after the catastrophe, an expedition led by L. Kulik arrived on the scene and penetrated deep into the fallen forest and undertook research work in the catastrophe area. The main discoveries were two notable observations:

A huge radial caving of the forest, all the trees pointed with their roots to the center of the explosion;

At the epicenter, where the damage from the fall of the huge meteorite should have been the greatest, the forest stood on its roots, but it was a dead forest: with the bark stripped off, without small branches... - The trees resembled telegraph poles stuck in the ground.

The reason for this could only be an above-surface explosion. It was also strange that in the middle of the dead forest there was water - a lake or swamp. Kulik immediately assumed that it was a crater formed by the fall of a meteorite.

During 1928, Kulik returned to the taiga with a major new expedition. Topographic photos of the area were taken, photographic and video footage was taken, and an attempt was made to pump water out of the craters using a self-contained pump. In the fall, several craters were dug up and magnetic measurements were taken, but no traces of a meteorite were found...

Kulik's third expedition in 1929-1930, was better equipped. They had special pumps for drying craters and drilling equipment at their disposal. They dried the largest crater, at the bottom of which a trunk was found, but it turned out to be older than the Tunguska event. And this meant that the craters were not meteoritic, but thermal in origin. It would follow that the meteorite or fragments of the meteorite simply... disappeared!

The failed expedition undermined Kulik's confidence in the iron meteorite hypothesis. He began to allow the idea that the "space visitor" might have consisted of stone. However, Kulik's faith in the iron meteorite was so strong that he did not even deign to look at the huge meteorite-like stone that was found by members of K. Jankowski's expedition. Attempts to find the "Jankowski stone", which lasted for 13 years, were not successful.

In 1938-1939, Kulik's last expeditions took place. Aerial photographs taken in 1938 of part of the area of the fallen forest yielded very valuable material, which was used for cartographic purposes. In the summer of 1939, Kulik spent the last time at the site of the TM fall. Under his leadership, work was carried out on the geophysical description of the area.

Kulik intended to send his next expedition in 1941, but World War II messed up his plans. So this is how the 1921-1939 expeditions to study the Tunguska problem went. This issue was taken up as early as 1949 by E.L. Krylov - a participant in Kulik's expedition and his student - in his book "Tungusskij Meteorit" he claims that TM was literally sprayed into the air on impact with the Earth, and that a swamp was created in the place of the post-impact crater. Krylov's book was published in 1952 and won the USSR State Prize.

2.2. The first fantastic versions

TM research was interrupted by the Great Patriotic War. It seemed that they would be quickly resumed after it, but life quickly brought its own adjustments to this.

On February 12, 1947, the great Sichote-Alinskiy Meteorite fell in the Far East, the study of which began immediately, and indeed - the researchers did not have enough strength and resources to work on two fronts. TP research was postponed indefinitely.

However, something unexpected appeared, something most unusual - and it happened because of one single publication. The thing was that in the January 1946 number of the magazine "Wokrug swieta", appeared a short story entitled "Wzryw"[16], author A. Kazantsev, who promoted the hypothesis that there was a nuclear explosion over the Tunguska taiga. What exploded was an extraterrestrial spacecraft... This version caused quite a buzz in the scientific world and caused a return of unprecedented interest in TM.[17]

It should be added here that Dr. Kazantsev was inspired by the first nuclear explosions over the Japanese cities of Hiroshima and Nagasaki in August 1945.[18] Kazantsev pointed out the following analogy: in Hiroshima, only those buildings survived that, paradoxically, were at the epicenter (or rather, under the epicenter) of the nuclear explosion, where the shock wave hit from above, exactly as seen in the Tunguska taiga. Just in the middle of the uproar of trees was a "dead forest of telegraph poles" - trees stripped of bark and branches - by the powerful blow of the shock wave. Kazantsev was stunned by one more thing: the similarity of the seismograms produced by the Tunguska explosion and the... Hiroshima and Nagasaki explosions!

---

[16] Wzryw (Russian) - explosion, blast.

[17] Who knows maybe the notorious "Roswell incident" was an American response to the fall of TM, which I will write more about in Part II of this study.

[18] The first nuclear explosion was the explosion of a load of uranium-235 at Jordana de Muerte (NM) on July 16, 1945, known by the code name *Trinity*.

After a fairly short period of time, Kazantsev's hypothesis was considered at a special meeting of the Moscow All-Union Astrogeodetic Society (WAGO), and later a paper was given at the Moscow Planetarium with staged demonstrations titled "Zagadka TM", which was delivered by astronomer Dr. F. Zigiel.

The hypothesis of an explosion that tore the alien spacecraft to pieces was first criticized by journalists and then also by scientists. Such specialists as A. Mikhailov, B. Vorontsov-Velyaminov, P. Parenago, K. Bayev and others took part in it. They noted, and justly admitted, that specialists in the field of meteoritology, instead of getting down to the task of verifying Kazancev's hypothesis and solving the TM problem, limit themselves to empty criticism and thus negate the achievements of Kulik's expedition.

Specialists-meteoritologists responded in an article by Prof. V. Fiesienkov and the secretary of the Committee on Meteorites of the AN of the USSR, Prof. E. Krinov, titled "Meteorite. "Meteorite ili marsjanskij korabl?"[19], in which the hypothesis of an artificial origin of the Tunguska phenomenon was debunked. The authors of the article wrote that it was not proven that the TP exploded in the air, and there is no mystery in the fall of the TM, and that everything is clear - it was a meteorite that fell and sank in the swamp, and the resulting post-impact crater was flooded by the softened swamp soil. And since no one was in the Tunguska taiga after Kulik's expeditions, the scientists' enunciations could not be based on some new material. Admitting that it was a nuclear explosion meant that it was an artificial body with all the resulting

---

[19] "Meteorite or Martian ship (spaceship)".

consequences, and such a step meteorologists would never allow themselves...

As it is colloquially said, the following detail added fuel to the fire - well, in 1957, an employee of the KM AN of the USSR, Dr. A. Yanwiel, discovered in soil samples brought by A. Kulik from the 1929-1930 expedition meteorite dust: particles of iron (Fe), with admixtures of nickel (Ni) and cobalt (Co), as well as microgranules of magnetite (Fe_3O_4) with a diameter of 0.01 mm - which are the product of the atomization of liquid metal in the air. Such pellets are found in the sputtering sites of iron-nickel meteorites, and they were particularly abundant at the site of the fall of the Sichote-Alinski Meteorite.

K. Staniukovich and E. Krinov immediately went to the press with the statement that this find provides a solution to the TM mystery. Supporters of the spaceship crash hypothesis, on the other hand, presented a set of found particles that matched them in composition not with an iron-nickel meteorite, but with the body and armor of a spaceship.

However, both came to be severely disappointed, and this was because the composition of these particles turned out to be misleading, as it turned out that the soil samples collected by Kulik had been "contaminated" with meteorite dust while they were resting in the storage facilities of the AN KM USSR - heavily dusted with space "dust". And to make things more interesting, a year later other Kulik's samples from the Khushma River expedition were analyzed, the iron balls were found there much less.

Due to the tumultuous development of Earth's cosmonautics and astronautics, as well as the exploration of the planets of the solar system with the help of automated probes, we have come to give up the hypothesis of the arrival of a spaceship to us from Mars or Venus.[20] The question of the origin of the post-impact crater in the so-called South Swamp required special treatment. A new expedition was needed.

After first completing the research work on the Sichotte-Alinsky Meteorite in 1947-1951, some researchers began to prepare for an expedition to the Podkamennaya Tunguska region, so in 1953 the Tunguska region was visited by geochemist Dr. K.P. Filorensky, but this was only a prelude, because the real research expedition set off into the taiga in 1958.

And here is an account from Kulik's expedition published in the Ogoniok magazine No. 49/1928:

Into the Taiga for the Meteorite

Diary and photos of expedition film operator N.A. Strukov

(The second expedition over the Podkamienaya Tunguska in 1927)

The past few months have passed in an atmosphere of nagging uncertainty about the fate of L.A. Kulik, who has undertaken a research effort in the midst of the uninhabited and wild taiga. A brief dispatch from Taishet announced for the USSR to the entire scientific world that the rescue expedition was announcing good

---

[20] Today, in the year 2023, it is not at all absolutely clear that there was no life on Mars at all, because some clues suggest the existence of life there, and even intelligent life!

news: Kulik found! [This is about the first reconnaissance expedition in 1921] Kulik rescued! Kulik is coming back! Who Leonid Kulik is and what his merits are, of course, many people know - this has been written about quite a lot in recent times. Let me just remind you of the main facts.

In 1908, from the deathless dark abyss of space, a huge meteorite mass fell to the surface of the Earth, unparalleled among other meteorites in the space of the present Earth civilization. It was something called the Tunguska Meteorite. It chose a deaf, uninhabited part of eastern Siberia as the site of its fall, and, unusual in its size and explosive power, the entire civilized world heard about this heavenly visitor. It heard and forgot...

The fact was that no one saw the meteorite fall, no one knew exactly where it fell, and no one went to look for it. The wild nomadic tribes of the Tunguska hunters saw only a fiery trail in the sky when it reached Earth, and soon they heard huge thunder-like sounds of explosions and an explosive cloud in the sky testifying, it was thought, that something had just fallen to Earth from the sky. Locals watched the enormous devastation of the taiga forest stand, the shockwave of the tree spreading for hundreds of kilometers from where it fell. Many deer lost their lives and in a hamlet called Kezhme, 360 kilometers from the site of the explosion, windowpanes flew out of the windows. The Tungusians fashioned a legend about the god of thunder who fell from the sky, and from then on they decided, fearing the wrath of this god, not to cross the border of the fallen and burned taiga.

In 1921, Leonid A. Kulik recalled the key facts of June 1908 from the darkness of oblivion and made a reconnaissance expedition, locating the site of the explosion, while in 1927 he had already decided to organize a special expedition to search for the Tunguska meteorite under his leadership. In the same year, thanks to the incredible energy of L.A. Kulik, the Russian Academy of Sciences and the Sownarkom of the USSR, a new expedition, already with extensive plans, was organized, which Kulik brought to a final stage with great difficulties. L.A Kulik's expedition did not delay setting out into the taiga, forgetting to take a cameraman with them. Only from Taishet, the last railroad station on the way to the site of the meteorite fall, was sent an urgent message to Sovkin: immediately send a film operator to Taishet - in the signature - Kulik. The trip falls on me. At an express pace, I prepared to go on a journey of 6,000 versts from Moscow into the unknown mysterious taiga, but happy that at least I was going to the people I knew from the search team, with whom I would soon have to walk hundreds of kilometers in the wilderness and shoot the scientific work with my camera on film. In the end, it turned out that not only did I come to work on the film like every member of the expedition on his task, but, like everyone else on the team, to do everything else that was needed at the time: the expedition leader worked as a porter, the cinematographer as a lumberjack, and so on.

The short telegram that summoned me on this incredible journey surprised me and more with the fact that the expedition had already left Taishet on its way without waiting for me, and I had to chase it alone in conditions that were really extremely difficult and even, I can honestly say, unimaginable for the average person. And I had hopes, which came to nothing, that I would meet the expedition in Taishet. At the local RIK they informed me that the expedition had gone into the taiga 5 days earlier ordering me to rent a horse and chase them. I faced the front of the wild taiga without any equipment to keep me alive - no weapons or similar equipment and in front of us (me and the horse) was 400 km of absolute wilderness. Exhausted, in the midst of the ice floes of already thawing rivers, crossing a mountain ridge still covered with snow, I found myself in a place where I should be dead. And we wandered fifty kilometers in snow up to our necks, on the leftovers of our strength, to finally reach a kinder road. With the last of our strength we reached the village of Dwór (Palace), located on the banks of the Angara - what irony in naming a wooden hut built of sparse sticks. There I stepped into the middle of the river, where the ice still held, and followed the sledge for 250 more kilometers to the hamlet of Kezhm. The ice was unsteady, and that's why it was sometimes necessary to put a boat on the sled and load the camera and film tape into it in case the sled went under the ice. From Kezhm on a barely visible deer trail with one worker hired there, six horses and three crates, I walked another 250 kilometers to the last point recorded on the maps - to Vanavara factories. There, 16 days after leaving Taishet, I doped the expedition. Vanavara factory was the last known civilized place there in this wilderness. Perched on the banks of the Podkamennaya Tunguska River, on the foothills of the impassable taiga, it consisted of three living compartments (huts?). When I crossed the river to Vanavara I was met by Leonid A. Kulik, and he was so incredibly overjoyed and happy and at the same time looking at me in disbelief that I had come here, that out of joy all the expedition participants danced some kind of incredible dance. Kulik confessed to me that he had absolutely not counted on me taking the risk of chasing the expedition through the unknown fateful wilderness and that he had succeeded in encouraging me to do so, and yet he continually came out of the hut and gazed at the place from where I should have come. I, on the other hand, became ill here. It was then that I first got to know him as a man who was unremarkable and relentless in his work.

When the ice thawed around the boats and they began to wobble on the water, he immediately ran along the bank of the Podkamennaya Tunguska River to look for and check the ice blockages to see if they had already drained and the river had been freed to move the boats. Meanwhile, I had recovered. The long-awaited moment when the river was cleared of ice and ice floes finally arrived, and then we were able to launch the boats - two light boats and one heavy cargo boat. Loaded with supplies and research apparatus, on May 22 we set off down the Podkamennaya Tunguska River supported by an agent from Vanavara and his family and the incumbent Tungush there. Together with us, that is me, Kulik, his helper Sityn and 5 workers, there were 8 of us in total. This is how we sailed, covering 30 kilometers, to the mouth of the Chambe River. The 2 horses we took could not pull our boats without being chased with a whip by Tropa, so the six of us slowed down the march. We barely managed to walk a kilometer in an hour. On this river 50 kilometers from its mouth, an accident occurred that nearly ended in the death of the expedition leader. Having reached the place where the river crossed a mountain peak and fell sharply from a mountain brink, we went ashore and pulled it by ropes. Two people remained in the boat, a worker - Angarec with a pole and L.A Kulik at the helm. I had already spread out on the bank with my camera and began to take pictures of this critical situation on the river through the stormy brink. Suddenly, in the worst place, the boat began to turn a whirlpool and tilted to the side, causing it to momentarily fill with water. The clever Angarec managed to jump onto the stone, but Kulik fell into the water. Caught by the water vortex, he went underwater twice, and inevitably would have died if he hadn't hooked his foot to some rope by the side, and if he hadn't had a life belt. I managed to record all this on tape. Watching this scene on the film, which was edited in Sovkino by director N.G. Vishnyakov, some viewers, perhaps, naively asked whether it was not staged? Well, but a close look at the situation as L.A. Kulik desperately fights against the deadly danger in the icy water under the agitated brink such speculation was to be dismissed.

This event did not affect L.A. Kulik in a negative way: having quickly changed his clothes, he proceeded to command the expedition with even greater energy. On the Chushma River, into the current of which we entered approximately 100 km from the mouth of the Chambe River, we began to be haunted by underwater rocks which, like guarded teeth, hammered into the bottoms of our boats, slowing our march. Having fallen from strength on these obstacles, about 70 km from the mouth of the river we were forced to leave some of our luggage. Near the mouth of the Churgima River, we camped at the same place where L.A. Kulik set up his thirteenth camp in 1921. There we set up our "inn" for fishing, (although at that time fish were in short supply), built a "łabaz" or food storage placed on four poles, and a banya (bathhouse) made of fallen trees. And from there we climbed up to the very spot where the meteorite hit. We built a road through the wetlands from fallen trees so that we could cross this swampy area. We walked 3-4 km a day so that the 12 km separating us from the epicenter of the explosion was covered in 4 days. In total, we walked from Vanavara to this point for 20 days and with rest stops for over a month. We reached our destination. In front of us stretched the mudflats and the place where the legendary fireball hit. The menacing "god of Thunder" lingered deep underground, and its explosive effect is still showing its effect, spreading over a great space. A fiery whirlwind over thousands of square kilometers licked away all vegetation - from bushes to century-old logs. The fallen forest spread before our eyes, we could already see it from above the Chambe River, from the same water threshold where L.A. Kulik experienced his dramatic adventure. The forest lies in rows of flat fallen trees, laid concentrically around the site of the meteorite fall and encircle the place as if it were so deliberately seeded Here there are neither animals nor bird. Delicate vegetation in places is beginning to revive from the conflagration, not a bit covering the battlefield and the effects of the deadly disaster. Twenty years ago, the entire lushly flourishing area turned into the kind of desert we still had before our eyes in the blink of an eye. The mountains surrounding the mudflats were also dead and bare. The meteorite itself could not be seen. He cut into the ground in pieces, and somewhere deep these parts lie, and this is reliably evidenced by dozens of huge craters carved into the surface of the muds, as after explosions. These craters are round and have a diameter of 5 to 50 meters and more. They have already managed to overgrow with mud grasses, which strangely enough sharply cut off in color from the surrounding vegetation. Therefore, when viewed from above, it presents an amazing sight.

At the edges of these mud ponds, it seemed that the ground was raised in accordance with the science of meteorites [xxxxx illegible 2 sentences from zdies-to to oszuszkatsja]. There were great difficulties in maintaining good quality food, especially essential vegetables in a situation of huge numbers of virulent mosquitoes and constant wading in water and swamps up to the knees. During the 18 days I stayed at the site of the meteorite fall, I had the opportunity to become closely acquainted with L.A. Kulik and his fanatical approach to science and all the companions of the expedition. I saw him demonstrate his human heroism in many cases. Kulik infected us with enthusiasm in the most difficult conditions, which for him seemed not to exist. Astonishingly, his vigor was not inferior to the native children of the harsh taiga. Worthy of the utmost attention in my eyes, what L.A. Kulik did was the decision to stay alone in the taiga. While sick, the other participants of the expedition were forced to return. Aide to the expedition chief Sytin, with his extensive expedition experience, was an extremely valuable associate of L.A Kulik in his work. Sytin's commitment was shared by everyone and me in particular. Sytin turned out to be an excellent not only geologist, but also a botanist, entomologist and also a cinematographer. Numerous examples of the expedition leaders' ingenuity infected all of us, too, who, not knowing the ins and outs of conducting research and scientific details, intuitively looked for all the details with the utmost care. A particular favorite of the expedition turned out to be the local young native Siberian we called Aleksis, whom I had brought with me from

Vanavara, and he proved to be a particularly useful helper. I consoled myself with the thought that this boy would soon come with Kulik to Moscow and see the Soviet capital he had dreamed of nostalgically at the time when he and I were wading through the Siberian expanses in those days.

Very difficult working and living conditions soon began to take their toll on our health, two workers fell ill with scurvy. The first signs of the disease appeared in me as well. When I finished my work, they had to send me and the other two sick workers away to save on meager food supplies.

On the way back, we encountered two additional jobs that had not yet been done on our first trip: first, bypassing ice-free rivers and second, meltwater. Having reached Kezhma, I busied myself with filming local nomadic life. Soon V.A. Sytin arrived in Kezhma with the rest of the workers, as they all fell ill as well. Thus L.A Kulik was left alone in the taiga. "Aleksis" clung to me and together we floated down the Angara to the Yenisei River where, in September, I changed to a steamship heading for Krasnoyarsk and on to Moscow. Sytin, with a rescue team, returned to Kulik, which, as it later turned out, he found quite quickly. Thus ended the expedition of Soviet scientists, which later turned out to be not as hype as the famous expeditions of Krasin and Maligin, but demonstrated before the world no less persistence in achieving the scientific goal, and nothing diminished its merits in the arduous and historic march north.

N. Strukow[21]

---

[21] Translated by Roman Rzepka. I received the material (in Russian) as a courtesy of Sergey Vasiliev - many thanks!

2.3. Further research

The study of the TM problem, according to Prof. Dr. N. V. Vasiliev - academician of the USSR AN, head of the KM of the Siberian Branch of the USSR AN and the Comprehensive Independent Expeditions Department - can be divided into several stages:

Stage one - began in the 1920s, is associated with the person of L. A. Kulik and his closest associates. Kulik's expeditions to the site of the TM fall have gone down in history forever, as an example of research courage and scientist's loyalty to a certain idea. Unfortunately, his fanatical devotion to the iron meteorite hypothesis prevented him from doing more comprehensive TP research.

Stage two - began in 1958. Here it is necessary to note the activity of K.P. Florensky, a student of Prof. V.I. Vernadsky. It was under his personal leadership that in 1958, 1961 and 1962 AN expeditions of the USSR went to the region of the TM fall. The 1958 expedition penetrated the extensive region of the forest overhang and made a detailed map of it. No post-impact craters were found either in the South Marsh or anywhere else. The thermal origin of the lakes in the quasi-craters was definitely proven. The metallic pellets found in the soil samples were no longer attributed to the meteorite: such pellets were also found under Moscow and under Leningrad[22] and in Antarctica, and

---

[22] St. Petersburg today.

even at the bottom of the World ocean. As it became clear, it was common cosmic dust and dust of terrestrial origin.

All the data collected by the Florensky expeditions showed that the TM did not reach the Earth's surface, but exploded in mid-air. No meteorite debris could be found in the area of the crash, but the expeditions discovered an abnormally rapid growth of trees in the area of the explosion.

Young scientists got to work. The youngsters could no longer be content with passive studies of known materials and the formulation of hypotheses. And it was for this reason that a group of students, aspirants and academics from Tomsk universities decided to undertake an expedition to the area of the Tunguska event. The leader of this group was a physicist and physician in one person - Prof. Dr. med. G. Plekhanov.

After short preparations, a group of 10 boys and 2 girls arrived at the site of the Tunguska event on June 30, 1959. This day became the day of the birth of the KSE (CIE) - Complex Independent Expeditions. The first expedition of the CIE had many goals to achieve and its activities were multifaceted: it carried out studies of the forest breakouts and the fire region, searched for meteorite remains, and carried out magnetometric and radiometric measurements. The latest expedition was led by Dr. A. Zolotov, a geophysicist from Bashkiria. Let me say right away that the exploration and research were not successful at first, but these expeditions set goals that are still being realized today. The CIE coordinates all the efforts of TM researchers in the USSR. Indeed, the CIE, is an informal organization that fills a huge interdisciplinary research program for a given problem, said CIE head Dr. N. Vasiliev.

The work was accelerated eminently in 1960, when parallel teams of the CIE worked together, a team of engineers from the Sergei Korolov Research Committee - which included the later cosmonaut G. Grechko - and the Zolotov group, whose program of works was developed by Professors L. Arcimovich, M. Kieldysh, E. Fedorov and others. From that year, the NPS received powerful support from the Siberian Branch of the USSR AN.

In 1961-1962, a new expedition headed by Dr. Florensky went to the site of TCB's fall. Members of the CIE worked together with members of other expeditions according to a unified program. The main results of the research carried out in 1958-1962 were:

1. Definitive determination of the area of forest caving;

2. Compilation of maps of the area of forest caving, the area of radiant burning, the "telegraphic forest" zone and the boundaries of the forest fire;

3. Confirm previous conclusions about the absence of post-impact craters and meteorite debris in the area;

4. To study the mutation of the vegetation cover and the acceleration of tree growth.

The second stage of TM's research in 1958-1962 made it possible to form a view of the physical nature of the Tunguska explosion, but the two most important problems: the mechanism of decay and the chemical composition of TCB still remained unsolved problems...

Stage three - lasted from 1964 to 1969. During this time, more operative and rigorous methods of separating cosmic dust from samples were worked out, and serious theoretical studies, including model tests, were made. In 1965, a momentous discovery was made that the caving of the forest in the region of the TP fall was caused not only by the explosion, but also by a ballistic shock wave. This discovery was confirmed already in the taiga and already in scientific laboratories. Field investigations carried out year after year have expanded our knowledge of the flash energy of the Tunguska explosion and its shock waves. All this has provided the theoretical basis for making an entry into the...

The fourth stage of research - in 1969, when the search, collection and analysis of micrometeorite dust in the area of the explosion, as well as data processing and synthesis of knowledge of the physics of the Tunguska explosion came to the fore. It should be said at this point that this stage continues to this day.

2.4. What do we know today?

To conclude this chapter, let us bring back a sufficiently brief and indeed incomplete characterization of the Tunguska event.

The nature of the explosion: it has been established that there is no post-impact crater at the site of the TM explosion - 70 km to the NW of the Vanavara factories, which astroblem[23] would have to occur in the event of a meteorite fall on the Earth's surface.

---

[23] Meteorite crater.

The above statement therefore suggests that the TCB did not reach the surface of our planet, but disintegrated or exploded at an altitude of 5 to 7 km. The explosion was not instantaneous; the TCB moved through the atmosphere, intensely ripping through as much as 18 km.

It should also be noted that TM "carried" into an unusual region - the region of former, extremely intense volcanism, with the epicenter of the eruption coinciding perfectly with... the center of the former crater! - The caldera of a giant volcano that was active in Triassic.[24]

Explosion energy: Most researchers of the catastrophe estimate its energy in the range of $10^{23} - 10^{24}$ ergs[25], which is equivalent to the explosion energy of 500 to as many as 2,000 Hiroshima-type A-bombs, or in TNT equivalent: 10 - 40 Mt TNT.[26] Part of this energy was transformed into a flash of light, while the remainder caused baryonic and seismic phenomena that were observed around the world...

---

[24] These are the so-called Tunguska Plateau or Tunguska Basalt Traps, which formed about 248 million years ago - that is, in the Upper Permian - and not in the Triassic, as the author states, and whose center is located at 70°N and 90°E. These volcanic traps are associated with one of the so-called "episodes of the Great Extinction" in Earth's history, the mechanism of which has not been explained to this day. It probably happened due to the impact of a high-mass meteorite or even an asteroid on the antipodes of this point, which caused the mass extinction of many species of flora and fauna.

[25] That is, $10^{17} - 10^{18}$ J (joules) in SI units.

[26] Some estimates are as high as 130 Mt TNT.

Mass of the meteorite: Many researchers put the mass of the meteorite in the range of 100,000 to 1 million tons. Recent calculations tend to favor the former number.

Image of a forest caving: The shock wave knocked down the forest massif over an area of 2,150 km². This surface is shaped like a butterfly sitting on the surface of the Earth, with the axis of symmetry oriented to the W or SW.

This image is specific. The forest is knocked down centrally, but unevenly.

Light flash energy: To understand the physics of the explosion, it is necessary to answer a fundamental question: how much of its energy is discharged as a flash of light? In researching this topic, scientists have turned their attention to long "blackeneds" - radiant burns on the bark of trees. The area of the taiga containing trees smeared in this way is about 250 square kilometers, and its contours resemble an ellipse - with a large half-axis exactly coinciding with the direction of the TM trajectory. The ellipsoidal shape of the radial burn area of the trees makes it possible to presume that the source of the intense light radiation, and thus also thermal radiation, was shaped like a droplet extended along the trajectory. The energy of the flash of light is estimated to have been 1,023 ergs, i.e. about 10% of the total energy of the explosion.

From the strong flash of light, the forest litter ignited. A fire broke out, differing from normal forest fires in that the forest ignited simultaneously over a large area, but the flames were battered by the blow of the shock wave. After that, the outbreaks of the fire were again revealed and the forest already knocked down was burning, with only the fires burning in the outbreaks, not the entire area.

Biological consequences of the explosion: they are related to changes in the speed of growth of trees - mainly pines - in the area of the catastrophe. A forest once grew there, the flora and fauna resumed their presence, however, in the area of the TP explosion the forest grows unbelievably fast, with not only the young trees, but also the 200-300 year old trees that survived after the TCB explosion. The maximum of such changes falls on a line coinciding with the TM trajectory! So it seems that the reason for this growth stimulation also exists today.[27]

What was this caused by? Is it just the fires that fertilized the soil with micro- and macronutrients that are plant growth stimulants? So far, these questions lack any answers!...

Flight trajectory parameters: In order to explain the physical processes that caused the explosion of the TCB, it is necessary to know what was the direction of its flight, as well as the angle of its trajectory relative to the plane of the horizon, and of course - its speed. According to all the data collected up to 1964, the TCB was traveling on an inclined trajectory, from south to north - in the so-called "Southern Variant". But after examining the forest overhang, scientists came to a second conclusion, namely - the trajectory of the TM was from E-SE to W-NW - that is, the so-

---

[27] An interesting constatation with observations of the behavior of plants at CE sites with UFOs arises here, and so in many cases there was also observed a tumultuous growth of plants at the sites of UFO landings in the following years, as was the case, for example, in Olsztyn near Częstochowa or Spytkowice.

called "Eastern Variant" appeared. In addition, immediately before the explosion, the TCB was moving exactly from E to W - the azimuth of the trajectory was 90-95°!

As the difference in direction of the two variants is 35°, then it can be assumed that the flight directions of TM during its arrival at the Earth's surface were changing!

Most TP researchers have concluded that the TM fell to Earth at an angle of 10-20° to the plane of the horizon. There is also talk of angles 30-35° and 40-45° - which leads us to believe that the angle of trajectory relative to the plane of the horizon also changed!

Also, estimates of TM's flight speed vary widely and boil down to two viewpoints, namely:

The flight speed of the TCB was 1 km/sec;

The flight speed of the TCB was 20 km/sec.

Meteorite remains: After the fact of the TM explosion over Earth was definitely confirmed, the search for debris lost its meaning, or at least the search for large pieces of TCB debris. The search for TM debris began in 1958 and continues to this day - without success.

The thing is that in the soils and peat of the crash area, five types of particles of cosmic origin have been discovered - silicon and iron-nickel particles in this number, however, it is impossible to relate them to TM in any way. They are nothing more than traces of past meteorite falls and cosmic dust fallout, which have been occurring daily since the dawn of the Earth and Solar System.

It should be taken into account here that there are former lava flows in the area, and that the dust created from the weathering of lava mixes with cosmic dust thus falsifying the picture of its distribution in the vicinity of the catastrophe

Geomagnetic effect: A few minutes after the explosion, a magnetic storm began, which lasted more than 4 hours. Such phenomena are observed in the atmosphere and magnetosphere of the Earth after high-altitude explosions of nuclear devices!...

The Tunguska explosion caused a brightly discernible polarization and magnetization of the soil within a radius of 30 km from the epicenter of the explosion. It's as if in this region the magnetization vector changed from north-south to south-north or disappeared altogether! What can cause such magnetic anomalies, no one knows to this day!!!

There are still two most important questions in the TM problem: How did it happen? and: What was it? The first question can be answered more or less based on previously collected and documented facts and materials, but the answer to the second question is not easy. In order to answer it, it is necessary to study many hypotheses, versions and proposals, which is the subject of the next chapter.

3. HYPOTHESES, INFORMATION, SUGGESTIONS.

3.1. After the golden jubilee

It is often said that more than a hundred hypotheses have already been formulated about the nature and origin of TM. In reality, there have never been these hundred hypotheses, because it is forbidden to elevate to the status of a scientific hypothesis some fantastic suggestions or even dreams related to TCB, and which are not confirmed in some way by facts, and there is no way to verify them.

In this case, one can only talk about a few - no more than three - hypotheses about the origin of TM, each of which has several variants, while all the rest are just versions and unverifiable ideas. The problem is that a scientific hypothesis, scholars believe, should meet two extreme criteria: primo - it does not contradict the facts and laws of modern knowledge, and secundo - it allows for the repetition of a given phenomenon and its full control. Of all the hypotheses to date, which we will consider in detail later in this work, only some pretend to be full-fledged theories. The rest, unfortunately, do not. Nevertheless, in the further part of this text I will use the terms "hypothesis" or "theory" to refer to the rest. We will consider the history of TM research in a time perspective. We will start with the 50th anniversary of the Tunguska event.

Wanting to intrigue readers, popularizers of the Tunguska issue placed emphasis on the ambiguities contained in it. From this the Reader got the impression that despite persistent efforts over 50 years of research nothing certain has yet been established. This is not the case, because based on the collected material one can confidently draw a picture of the physical mechanism of the Tunguska explosion and pronounce on its, for example, meteoritic origin and nature. At the same time, it should be noted that in the pre-war and post-war years this view has not lost its relevance.

It was believed that TCB was a huge iron or stone meteorite that fell to the Earth's surface in the form of one or more lumps. Such a view persisted until 1958, although Kulik's expeditions had already demonstrated the incorrectness of this viewpoint. According to this hypothesis, there should have been an astroblem at the epicenter of this explosion, which, as we know, could not be found...

The research of 1958-1959 led to the conclusion: the explosion occurred not on Earth, but in its atmosphere. In 1962, during the expedition of Filorensky (AN USSR) and Plekhanov (KSE), it became obvious that the post-impact crater was not there. Thus, it was proven that the explosion took place 5 - 7 km above the taiga, which was in no way connected with its meteoritic origin. It would seem, therefore, that the meteorite hypothesis has been a complete failure, but... let's take our time. We will return to it later in this work.

Among the numerous hypotheses about the nature of TM, the most reliable is the hypothesis of its cometary origin, which was first formulated in 1934 by English meteoritologist Dr. F.

Whipple, followed by Prof. I. Astapovich of the USSR. However, when we get acquainted with the book by American astronomer H. Shapley entitled "From the Atom to Milky Ways" (1930), we will find in it the proof that in 1908 the Earth collided with comet P/Pons-Winnecke[28]. The supposition of a collision with a P/Pons-Winnecke comet was put forward by Kulik back in 1926, but the hypothesis was not confirmed and the first TP researcher distanced himself from it.

In 1961-1964, the cometary hypothesis was dusted off and refined by Prof. V. Fiesenkov, claiming that an undersized comet exploded in the Tunguska taiga and entered the dense layers of the Earth's atmosphere at tremendous speed. Going by Fiesienkov's premise, well-known gasodynamicist Dr. K. Staniukovich and Associate Professor V. Shalimov worked out the pattern of the thermal explosion of the comet's icy nucleus. They interpreted the explosion as the result of melting and evaporation of cometary ice, which perfectly explained the lack of astroblems and larger debris of TCB.[29]

Looking from the point of view of the cometary hypothesis, Fiesienkov also explained the night sky glow in July 1908. It could have been caused by the sputtering of the comet's tail (pigtail) in the atmosphere, whose particles were deflected westward by the

---

[28] The distinction P stands for "periodic".

[29] In 2000, a theory of the origin of the so-called "pearl clouds" appeared, which explains their formation at heights of 20-25 km above Earth precisely by falling into the atmosphere of our planet small comets. So it would seem that the comet responsible for the TP was not so small, but quite the opposite!

solar wind. True, and in this case it was not possible to explain all the physical effects, ot, for example, the physical mechanism of the explosion was not fully explained.

That's why attempts were made to explain the nature of TM from non-traditional positions, first in popular literature and then in scientific literature. Thus, for example, the well-known geophysicist Dr. A. Zolotov, who visited the TP site several times, developed a hypothesis that the TM explosion was not chemical, but nuclear - and which was published in "Referees of the AN of the USSR" vol. 136, no. 1,1961 and in the monograph "The Problem of the Tunguska Catastrophe" published in 1970.

Beginning in the 1960s, Zolotov conducted TM research according to a program drawn up by several academic scientists. They examined slices of wood stripped from the trunks of Tunguska trees. It turned out that the jars of trees that survived the Tunguska event contained a much higher amount of radioactive material than those from before 1908 - but without looking at the fact that TM from the point of view of the amount of energy released can be compared to a nuclear or even thermonuclear explosion, no traces of radioactive fall-out after 1908 were found. Several scientists have made a number of tests with instruments much more sensitive than those used by Zolotov and have not confirmed his results. This means that the TCB explosion exposed the tree to a dose of radiation, but there was no radioactive fallout, as after a nuclear explosion. The nuclear explosion hypothesis does not explain the "white nights" phenomenon in the summer of 1908 at all, and it is difficult to associate the TM explosion with nuclear explosions known to science.

In addition, a group of Tomsk physicists and doctors reviewed the archives of the city's hospitals, questioned witnesses to the explosion, including the oldest residents and doctors, and exhumed Ewenks who died after 1908. No traces of unknown (radiation) diseases were found, and no decay products were found in the skeletons of these Ewenks either. All these facts again contradicted the nuclear explosion hypothesis.[30]

In addition to these main hypotheses, a variety of fantastic ideas and proposals proliferated throughout the 1960s. There were so many of them that it is impossible to talk about them even briefly. Therefore, we will move on to the next paragraph - to the 60th anniversary of TM.

3.2. Over sixty years

In this paragraph we will deal with a retrospective review of materials from the domestic and foreign press from 1969-1978. It contains hypotheses and versions (not all of them, of course - there was a terrible amount of it) attempting to explain from different positions the event of 1908, and which, according to the author of this work - are also interesting to this day.

---

[30] Nuclear explosion of atomic and hydrogen bombs. However, it is suspected that this could have been a "pure" explosion, i.e., the product of which is only radiant energy (thermal, light, X- and γ-rays) and mechanical energy (shock waves), which is exactly what was observed in 1908. Another possibility would be a fuel-air explosion (thermobaric bomb).

3.3. Whether the maneuver over Tunguska was executed?

An article by Doc F. Zigiel appeared in "Tiechnikie Mołodioży" No. 7,1969, in which he posed a question about the two trajectories of TM flight. He writes in it the following:

Based on eyewitness testimony and hyperseismic (earthquake) data, the "southern variant" was most convincingly justified by Prof. I. Astapovich. According to the testimony, it came out that the azimuth of this variant of the trajectory exceeded 10° west of the meridian.[31] This result matched perfectly with the earlier findings of A. Voznesensky and L. Kulik, which were made on the «warm footprint» of the crash.

Initially, the « southern variant» of the trajectory was considered the most reliable, but when every hectare of the site was carefully examined, it was unexpectedly clarified that the azimuth of the flight direction was not 10°W, but as much as 115°E from the meridian! This was clear from the study of the position of the trunks on the ground, which, as is well known, were overturned by the explosion and ballistic wave.

In order to explain the physical processes that the TCB explosion caused, it is necessary to know what was the angle of the TM trajectory to the plane of the horizon. Let me say right away - both in the «southern» and «western» variants it did not exceed 10°.

---

[31] This meant that TM flew a course of 350° from south to north with a ten-degree west declination.

In their time, I. Zotkin and M. Cikulin conducted a series of experiments, as a result of which they obtained a convergence in the contours of the destroyed forest zone at an angle of inclination close to 30°. Again, something does not add up. Thus, it looks like the TCB made maneuvers both in azimuth and elevation during its flight, moving not along a ballistic curve - like any "honest" meteorite or missile, but at a variable speed, and thus with a variable trajectory. The two "western" and "southern" trajectories are in no way mutually exclusive. Apparently, as Zigiel believes, the TM was moving along these trajectories, because somewhere it performed a maneuver.

But such a maneuver a natural object could not perform! Therefore, if the hypothesis of a transition from one trajectory to another is correct, it becomes a decisive argument for the artificial origin of TCB!

3.4. Tunguska meteorites fall every year!

An important contribution to the determination of the origin and nature of the TM is the findings reported by the scientific officer of the Meteorite Committee, Dr. I.G. Zotkin, which he made public in the magazine "Priroda" in 1971:

Recently, thanks to the expansion of the network of seismometric and barometric stations[32] , dozens of bolide

---

[32] In the USSR and the U.S., such stations were used to record the waves generated by nuclear tests on the territory of other countries, which allowed

overflights have been recorded which manifested their presence with audiovisual effects and left no meteorites behind.

On March 31, 1965, at 9:47 p.m. local time, a spherical bolide[33] glowing with blinding light flew from east to west over southern Canada. Its flight ended with a thunderous explosion that could be heard at least 200 kilometers away. A vortex of fiery debris scattered over the small town of Reveltown. Seismic stations in neighboring provinces recorded an unexpected earthquake of medium strength. As for the shock wave, infrasound microphones picked up its presence even in California, i.e. at a distance of 1,600 km from the epicenter!

The persistence of the searchers was rewarded - in April, several fragments weighing less than one gram each were found on the ice cap of a small lake. The meteorite turned out to be of a rare species - carbonaceous chondrite - well, and the question remained: what happened to the main mass of the meteorite???...

Recalling similar accidents is unnecessary. Recall that such events have been occurring for decades and have their analogy to TM. Seismic and barometric stations record such incidents many times a year. It turns out that in the Earth's atmosphere from time to time thunder explosions of space projectiles - true - their caliber is many times smaller than TM.[34] The important thing is that the explosion of cosmic bodies that invade the Earth's

the control of nuclear potential and compliance with collective security agreements, especially during the Cold War period.

[33] In the original "szarowoj (spherical) bolid".

[34] A similar phenomenon was last recorded over New Zealand on July 7, 1999, at 03:15 GMT.

atmosphere is more typical than the falling into it of "normal" meteorites. Only massive iron and stone meteorites reach the Earth's surface, with relatively low speeds - no more than 20 km/s. In addition, the entry corridor for entering and flying through the Earth's atmosphere is relatively narrow. Perhaps, the largest part of the meteorites are fast, crushed, containing the most carbon and water or organic compounds in their mass? Or could it also be a fast ball of snow from frozen gases and (water) ice? If so, then there is no issue with the TM problem. As for the energy and mechanism of bolide explosions, they are clear and understandable enough. The enormous kinetic energy of the bolide - at a speed of 30 km/s - 1 kg of its mass carries an energy equal to 100 Mcal or 100 times more than 1 kg of TNT. Already at an altitude of 20 km above the Earth, the jet of compressed air velocity can literally crush the meteorite into a pancake. The plane of attack will increase by this, and the air resistance can stop the meteorite, while the energy of motion will transform into thermal and light radiation and shock waves, and this means an explosion... Does this mean that TMs fall to Earth in every case!

It can't be said that Dr. Zotkin's article passed unnoticed. Well, but his summary - as you can see - was not carefully read by many TCB researchers. Such a situation still prevails today.[35]

---

[35] In Poland, we also have had several events that cannot be explained as well as TM. These are: The Great Polish Bolide of August 20, 1979, which flew over the entire territory of Poland from Rozewie to Solina, and while flying maneuvered in the air like a flying ship, and the so-called Jerzmanowice Meteorite, which on the evening of January 14, 1993 swept off the top of Babia Góra in Jerzmanowice near Kraków. Both of these accidents may have been caused by cosmic bodies, but so far no one has proved this directly...

3.5. The Tunguska comet: truth or myth?

Another "contribution to the basket" of cometary hypotheses about the origin and nature of the TM became the publication in the magazine "Tiechnika Młodiоżу" No. 9/1977 of an article by S. Goleniecki and V. Stepanek. Counting that the main mass of the TM escaped in the form of vapors and gases, the authors proposed searching not for meteorite particles, but simply for anomalies in the chemical composition of soils taken at the site of the crash. But where to look for them?

Statements from the few eyewitnesses to the catastrophe who were near the epicenter of the crash on that fateful day state that they heard not one, but up to five relatively powerful explosions.

Well, but neither a nuclear, let alone thermonuclear, explosion can occur twice, let alone five times! Besides, the series of explosions announcing the fall of the TCB, could have taken place at low altitude, and thus there could have been "dirt" on the Earth's surface from the products of the explosion and dust from TM decay. And this, in turn, would mean that the image of this explosion was not a single, but a "fivefolde", and therefore the remains of TCB should be looked for in the epicenters of such low, above-ground explosions!

It should also be mentioned here that even Kulik and Krinov pointed out that the image of the destruction at the center of the

Both of these cases are still open to this day!

catastrophe has a kind of "five-point" character. In his book "Tungusskij meteorit" Krinov writes that:

It could be assumed that the blast wave had a radial character and seemed to "capture" separated areas of the forest where it caused a caving or other damage.

Golenetskiy, Stepanok, together with Kolesnikov, proceeded to implement their idea, especially since one of the Tomsk researchers of the Tunguska problem, Y. Lvov, found a perfect way to do it: well, the discovered peat bogs turned out to be perfect traps for cosmic and atmospheric dust, preserving it in their layers as it successively fell into them. There are more than enough such peat bogs in the catastrophe area, and one of them was located in the center of the forest dump, as Kulik already knew. And it was here that the authors of this hypothesis examined a set of peat samples taken from various depths. In doing so, they used state-of-the-art methods of chemical and physical microanalysis.

At a certain depth corresponding to the layer that formed at the time of the disaster and later became overgrown with moss, the researchers discovered anomalously high concentrations of many chemical compounds.

And this is how, according to Golenetskiy and Stepanok, they were able to obtain the approximate chemical composition of the dust formed from the smashed TCB explosion. The chemical composition of this dust turned out to be unusual and clearly sharply cut off from the background chemical composition of peat and its "earthly" admixtures and impurities, as well as from meteorites: stone as well as iron. The composition resembled most the composition of carbonaceous chondrites - not very well known and quite rare, and rich in carbon and other volatile substances.

The results of the research and the data obtained - as the authors of the article think - make it possible to no longer make assumptions, but to prove outright that TCB was indeed a comet nucleus. And this allowed to explain the causes of many phenomena that followed the fall of TM. And so, for example, the increased growth of the forest after the catastrophe, in addition to purely ecological reasons, can be explained by the post-explosion fallout of a large amount of "mineral fertilizers" from the comet nucleus, biologically important micro- and macro-elements for plant life.

In conclusion, I will say that this hypothesis has provoked a wide response: Dr. V. Bronstein rated it extremely highly in his article in "Tiechnikie Mołodioży" No. 9/1977, while Doc. F. Zigiel sharply and negatively evaluated it in the pages of "Tiechniki Mołodioży" No. 3/1979.

3.6. Hypotheses of the 1980s: So a meteorite?

We extend a retrospective review of the numerous hypotheses about the nature and origin of the TP that saw the light of day already in our years, i.e., in the penultimate decade of the 20th century...

In "Tiechnikie Mołodioży" No. 11/1981, the original hypothesis of Dr. N. Kudryavtsevtsev on the geological nature of the Tunguska event was presented, which, according to the Author of this version, turned out to be a manifestation of... water-mud volcanism!...

A geological survey of the vicinity of the Tunguska event shows that there are former volcanic chimneys in the vicinity of Vanavara, while the Tunguska Basin itself is an area of deep underground basaltic rocks - batholiths - covered by thick stratified and volcanic sediments. The black mud filling the bottoms of the craters is of volcanic origin, but it is permeated with organic compounds on which all kinds of vegetation grows rapidly.

And it is the South Marsh - located in a basin surrounded by hills, according to a statement by Ewenk, who lived there until the catastrophe - that was previously hard ground. Reindeer walked on it and did not sink into the mud - he declared.[36] But after the explosion there was water, which like fire both man and wood eats away!

According to Kudriavtsevoy, the connection of the catastrophe with the fall of the meteorite turns out to be a mere conjecture, which was taken on faith all the more so because at the very beginning of the catastrophe a flying fireball was seen in the sky and thunderous rumbles sounded at its appearance in the sky. Given the difference in the speed of travel of sound and light, it must be believed that the source of these rumbles began before the bolide's light appeared.

Then, judges Kudriavtsevoy, there was an explosion shortly before the appearance of the meteorite's fireball in the sky and a fire occurred. It should be further noted that the burns on the old trees are visible only on some parts of the tree trunks, which openly contradicts the fact that the embers came from above, from the fireball.[37]

Geology knows of many cases of volcanic eruptions whose course is identical to that of the Tunguska event. As for the strength of the eruption, the most similar to the Tunguska explosion is the eruption of Krakatoa volcano (Rakata)[38] near Java, which took place in August 1883, and as for the composition

---

[36] This is not an argument in favor, because the hoof structure of reindeer and American caribou allows them to walk freely in the swamp!

[37] The above works only for dense spruce crowns, but not for sparse pine crowns, which transmitted the radiation of the light and thermal pulse of the explosion!

[38] Not true: the TM explosion released only 1 EJ, while the Krakatoa explosion released as much as 3 EJ - or 3×10^{18} J - of energy!

of eruption products, mud volcanic eruptions from Azerbaijan, which are associated with deep-sea magmatic geological processes. Thus, volcanism in the area of the Tunguska event may have manifested as a mud-gas eruption with the ejection of volcanic mud on the surface: water + volcanic rocks fragmented by the explosion[39], and therefore the Tunguska event may have been a demonstration of volcanism from ancient geological eras.[40]

Sufficiently close to this hypothesis of Dr. Kudriavtsev is the proposal put forward by Krasnoyarsk resident D. Timofeyev on the causes of the Tunguska explosion. He believes - in the pages of "Komsomolskoj Prawdy" issue of October 8, 1984 - that the cause of the explosion was the most ordinary natural gas. Assuming that there are deposits of natural gas underground in the area of the catastrophe, then due to the underground shock this gas could have been released into the atmosphere... Timofeyev calculated that for an explosion with a power equal to that of Tunguska's, 0.25 - 2.5 billion cubic meters of natural gas would first have to be released into the atmosphere. Looking at it from the point of view of geology, this magnitude is not so huge at all...

The gas escaped from the ground and the wind carried it around the eruption site. In the higher layers of the atmosphere, the gas mixed with ozone and slowly oxidized, and that's how the

---

[39] The explanation may be much simpler: the shockwave of the explosion caused the crushing of the upper layer of soil and volcanic rocks, which then soaked up the subsoil water, resulting in the formation of a swamp.

[40] A similar phenomenon can hardly be assumed to have occurred in the area only once and never before or later, which puts the whole hypothesis under a powerful question mark...

glow appeared in the sky. During the day the gas train should reach a length of 400 km. After mixing with the air, the gas should turn into a huge cloud, threatening to explode at any moment. All it took was a single spark, and... A few dozen kilometers away from Tunguska, the gas train entered the zone of the atmospheric front. Like a giant bolide, the front of the explosion wave of the ignited lightning mixture rushed north. In the basin, where the concentration of gas was greatest, a huge flaming ball formed. The explosion shook the taiga. The impact of the blast wave of the explosion closed the outlets of the natural gas and it stopped escaping into the atmosphere. Timofeyev even explained the observation made by the Ewenks after the catastrophe: the water in the swamp burned like fire. After all, the composition of natural gas includes, among other things, hydrogen sulfide (H2S). As it burns in the air, it produces sulfur oxide, and this mixed with water gives sulfuric acid. This hypothesis would explain a lot...[41]

---

[41] Unfortunately, this hypothesis does not explain anything, because it is difficult to assume that the gaseous train dragged continuously for half a thousand kilometers and did not encounter a fire source, not to mention the fact that methane forms a lightning mixture in the air, which can explode even from sunlight or a mere spark. Also, the sulfuric acid maelstrom is pure fiction, since hydrogen sulfide burned in the air oxidizes only to water and sulfur dioxide, according to the reaction:

1. $H_2S + 1\frac{1}{2}O_2 \rightarrow H_2O + SO_2$

which products combining together give sulfuric acid according to the reaction formula:

2. $H_2O + SO_2 \rightarrow H_2SO_3$

falling on the ground in the form of so-called "acid rain" - as every ecologist knows. The fallout from such rain would have destroyed huge areas of taiga. Meanwhile, the taiga grew itself, and much better than before the explosion! Thus, there could not be sulfuric acid in the slough, because sulfur dioxide is

And finally, we will quote the last version, which is very close to both of the above mentioned here. It first saw the light of day in August 1989, and was published by a special correspondent of the newspaper "Sowieckaja Rossija", editor N. Dombkovskiy.

And it was like this: in the area of the epicenter of the Tunguska explosion, where quite recently geologists discovered rich deposits of gas hydrate[42] a large amount of gas leaked through the cracks, forming an explosive cloud of lightning mixture. In the morning, a bolide lit to white accidentally fell into this cloud. A monstrous explosion blasted the bolide itself to dust and killed everything living around it...

---

very reluctant to oxidize to sulfur trioxide, and this process is basically impossible without a catalyst (di-vanadium pentoxide or platinum) and temperatures of the range +400...+500°C, which proceeds according to the equation:

3. $SO_2 + \frac{1}{2}O_2 \rightarrow SO_3$ (presence of a catalyst V_2O_5 or Pt and t = +400-500°C)

and then combines with water to form sulfuric acid according to the reaction equation:

4. $H_2O + SO_3 \rightarrow H_2SO_4$.

We can hardly suppose that such a complicated process could take place in nature, without catalysts and sufficiently high temperatures, well, unless we assume that a meteorite made of vanadium and platinum oxides fell there???...

[42] Some gases from the group of light hydrocarbons such as methane - CH4, ethane - C2H5, propane - C3H10, butane - C4H13, ethylene - C2H2 or acetylene - C2H4, when subjected to a pressure of 30-40 MPa and a temperature of +4°C, form compounds called hydrates with seawater. NB, it is most likely that hydrate deposits in the Bermuda Triangle and the Dragon Triangle are responsible for the strange phenomena occurring there.

A picture similar to what happened in the Podkamennaya Tunguska region, the author saw from a helicopter, in Bashkiria in 1989:

...The explosion of the gas cloud, which ruptured from the gas pipeline, caused the deaths of hundreds of people and destruction very similar to that of 1908... Also, the testimony of eyewitnesses to the event coincided in detail with descriptions of the Tunguska explosion... Entirely![43]

A comparison of the mechanisms of the explosion under Ufa with those of the Tunguska event showed their complete similarity. In addition, the explosion of the methane hydrate deposit explains many phenomena in and around the epicenter of the explosion.[44] According to Dombkowski's views, when a flared cosmic body fell into a gaseous cloud, its explosion began at the periphery, in these places the concentration of gas is low and a lightning mixture is formed. The explosion proceeded

---

[43] Similar explosion effects were observed in a gas pipeline explosion in Nachitoches (LU, USA), on March 4, 1965, where the fiery cloud reached temperatures of more than 1,000°C and reached a height of 200 meters. The catastrophe resulted in the loss of 17 lives. The flash of the explosion was seen from 100 km, while the shock of the explosion was felt from 50 km. A similar event occurred on March 12, 2001 at around 19:30 GMT about 200 km west of Moscow, where a gas pipeline exploded and caught fire. Again, the column of smoke reached 11,000 meters and the seismic shock of the explosion was recorded in Helsinki. The number of deaths and property damage is still unknown. Something like this can be compared to the spatial explosion of a thermobaric bomb.

[44] Also in the Bermuda Triangle and the Dragon Triangle there are explosions of methane hydrate deposits, what the Americans call "blue thunder" and the Japanese call "uminari".

detonationally. Having enveloped the gas cloud at the periphery, the explosion then enveloped the remaining mass of gas - this was also an explosion, but no longer detonational. The column of fire, the radial howl of the forest and the bare trees standing at the epicenter can be explained with this.

What can be said about these versions? For all their boldness and courage and originality of outlook, they do not - unfortunately - answer many of the main questions of the problem. They do not explain, for example, that the explosion was not instantaneous: the TCB moved exploding over at least 15-20 km!

3.7. The trace leads to the Sun

In the early 1980s, the scientific staff of the Siberian Branch of the USSR's AN: Dr. A. Dimitriev and Dr. V. Zhuravlev presented the hypothesis that the TM was a de facto plasmid, a creation that broke away from the Sun...

Humanity has long been acquainted with mini-plasmids - ball lightning - although their nature has not been fully investigated to this day. Astrophysicists are familiar with giant galactic plasmids. And here is one of the latest news of science: The Sun turns out to be a generator of colossal plasma formations with almost zero density.

Indeed, modern cosmophysics admits the possibility of considering our Solar System as a material-field structure whose stability is sustained not only by the law of universal gravity, but also by energy-information relationships. One of the concrete results of the interaction between the Earth and the Sun may be cosmic bodies of a new type, coronal densities, the model of which was proposed by geophysicist Dr. K. Ivanov.

Dimitriev and Zhuravlev, in their hypothesis, allow the possibility of the existence in the Cosmos of so-called "micro-densities" of medium size - plasmatic bodies with sizes ranging from tens to hundreds of meters in diameter. The considered "micro-plasmoids" or "energospheres", i.e. energy carriers from interplanetary space, can be intercepted by the Earth's magnetic field and drift along the lines of force of its magnetosphere. To make things more interesting, they can fly into regions of magnetic anomalies. It is incredible that such a plasmid could reach the Earth's surface without exploding in its atmosphere. As proposed by Dimitriev and Zhuravlev - TCB was among just such plasmids that broke away from the Sun.

One of the main arguments "against" the Tunguska problem is the issue of the variability of the TM trajectory. Dimitriev and Zhuravlev took all the accounts of the TP flight and plugged them into a computer. And what did they find out? Namely, it turned out that the partisans of the "southern" and "eastern" orientations were right, and that's because there was as much at stake here as two meteorites! Traditional meteoritics pas before such a "split" TM in time and space. Could it be that as many as two huge meteorites have set a randez-vous at the same point in space-time! Well, yes but Dimitriev and Zhuravlev see nothing unusual in this, if one allows the plasmid hypothesis. After all, it turns out that galactic plasmids "have a habit" of existing in pairs. This property also belongs to solar plasmids!

It appears that on June 30, 1908, as many as two fiery objects descended toward Earth over eastern Siberia. At least two! When the atmosphere of our planet became denser, this "celestial duo" exploded... The above becomes the starting point for a scientific discussion of the origin of the TP.[45]

There is another "solar" hypothesis regarding TM, which was presented by mineralogist Dr. A. Dimitriev in the pages of Komsomolskaya Pravda in the June 12, 1990 edition.

The fantasists have not yet discovered the relationship between ozone holes and TP, although in some popular science publications, such as "Winownica ziemnych bied?"[46] from the series "Znak woprosa" No. 7, 1990, tried to connect these unusual events together into a logical whole.

Severe atmospheric ozone depletion has already been observed in Earth's history, so a group of scientists led by Prof. K. Kondratiev recently published the results of their research, according to which in April 1908 a significant destruction of the ozone layer was observed at mid-latitudes of the Northern Hemisphere. This stratospheric anomaly, the width of which was 800-1,000 km, girdled the entire globe. This was the case until June 30, after which the ozonosphere returned to normal!...[47]

---

[45] Solar plasmids, NB, which no one has seen or caught, have recently been accused by Prof. Dr. Janusz Gil in his book "UFO, Däniken i zdrowy rozsądek" (Warsaw 1996) of moving through the atmosphere already singly or in groups, and creating for observers a phenomenon known as UFOs... - which I leave without comment.

[46] "The culprit of the earth's misfortunes?"

[47] And yet it should be the other way around, since the emission of greenhouse gases and post-impact dust should just cause or exacerbate the

Isn't this a strange coincidence of two important physical and chemical events for the planet? What was the nature of the mechanism that restored this delicate balance to normal? Answering these questions - as Dimitriev believes - we can say that the threatening lack of ozonosphere on Earth was responded to by... The sun! A large density of solar plasma, which has ozonogenic properties, was ejected from the Sun in the direction of our planet. This density met the Earth in the region of the East Siberian Magnetic Anomaly. According to Dimitriev, the Sun will not allow "ozone starvation" on Earth. So it seems that the more intensively Humanity destroys the ozonosphere, the more intensively the Sun will send gas-plasma-type creations towards us... One does not need to be a prophet to imagine what this could end. The scenario of the development of events on our planet, which is permanently "frequented" with plasma "gifts" from the "thinking" about the Earth Sun is not difficult to predict - it is enough to recall what happened in the Tunguska taiga on the last day of June 1908...

3.8. Information "container"?

effect of the already existing ozone hole! So far, it is the ozone hole effect that is mainly caused by carbon halides, or CFCs: CF_3Cl, CF_2Cl_2, CCl_3F and CF_4 - which break down ozone - O_3 into "ordinary" oxygen - O_2. Where did freons come from in the atmosphere in April 1908? - That's what no one knows so far...

The idea about the artificial origin of the Tunguska explosion has found and still finds its supporters over the years. Out of chronicling duty, I note that here and there new "evidence" for its confirmation keeps appearing. Confirmation of the above turns out to be the version of physicist Dr. A. Prijma published in "Tiechnikie Mołodioży" No. 1/1984.

In his considerations, Dr. Prijma refers to the information Ing. A. Kuzovkin gave during a round table - a panel discussion organized by the editors of "Tiechnikie Mołodioży" in October 1983.

Based on the testimony of witnesses to the anomalous atmospheric phenomena in 1908, Kuzovkin stated that the TM had, as it turns out, a "western" trajectory as well. In other words, the TCB flew not only from south to north, east to west, but also from west to east!!! Witnesses recounted that smaller copies of the TCB were observed in the first half of 1908 over settled areas of Russia, the Urals and Siberia.

According to Prijma, the fact of finding the western trajectory of the TM proves that there was not, as F. Zigiel believes, a maneuver of only one single object, but only a maneuver of three different bodies! It can be assumed that the "fireballs" flew over the pre-planned regions of our planet and then "came together" over the Podkamiennaya Tunguska to merge into one flaming object and explode!!! What follows, the Tunguska explosion may have been - according to Prijma - a deliberate action of the Non-Earthly Mind...

It is interesting that this "search for each other" of fireballs went from populated places towards more unpopulated ones and their randez-vous took place over completely unpopulated areas - it would seem that the place of the fall was inadvertently chosen so as to reduce the risk of killing people to zero.

The author of the quoted version is convinced that the TCB itself was not completely destroyed and certainly went into a "new stage of existence", i.e. changed its physical and chemical structure. So what happened? perhaps TM was an artificial "container" with some information that an unknown Extraterrestrial Civilization saw fit to send to our biosphere, and perhaps even to us. It will all be revealed when we are ready to receive this information!

And what happens if this "information field" from this TCB "container" is a constant, and we - Earthlings - bathe all day long in this "information soup" that has been cooked for us somewhere out there, in a distant other world? Perhaps the discharge of "information containers" into the middle of a developing civilization - which we consider ourselves to be - is one of the goals of accelerating their development on all the planets of our Universe?... Maybe this process is permanent throughout the Cosmos?... Who knows the answer to all these questions???!!!...

3.9. "Ricochet"

An original hypothesis that explains some of the astonishing consequences of TM's fall was put forward by Leningrad scientist Prof. Dr . E. Yordanishvili and published in "Literaturnoj Gazietie" in the April 25, 1984 edition.

It is known that the body, which entered the Earth's atmosphere at speeds of tens of kilometers per second, "ignites" at an altitude of 100-130 km. However, a significant number of witnesses to the fall of the TCB were in the Angara basin, i.e. at a distance of several hundred kilometers from the site of the crash, taking into account the curvature of the Earth's surface, we conclude that we cannot observe the course of the event unless we assume that the TM ignited at an altitude of no less than 300-400 km! So how to explain the glaring discrepancy between theoretical considerations and observed facts? The author of the hypothesis tried to prove his conjecture without leaving the frame of reality and without contradicting the rules of Newtonian mechanics.

Prof. Yordanishvili believes that on that unforgettable morning for many people, a celestial body came towards the Earth, which entered the atmosphere of our planet at a small angle. At an altitude of 120-130 km it lit up, and its huge glowing "tail" was seen by hundreds of people from Baikal to Vanavara. Coming into contact with the Earth, the meteorite "ricocheted" -

and jumped up several hundred kilometers - which is why it was also seen over the Angara River. Then TM described a parabola and lost its cosmic speed, and then fell to Earth - this time for good...

The hypothesis of an ordinary ricochet, well known to us from a school physics course, allows us to explain a whole series of consequences: the appearance of a glowing body above the limits of our atmosphere, the absence of astroblems and debris of TM at the site of its first "encounter" with Earth, the phenomenon of the so-called white nights in 1908 caused by the ejection into the atmosphere - and into the ionosphere - of Earth soil particles by TCB, etc. Besides, the cosmic ricochet hypothesis explains another ambiguity - the strange "butterfly" shape of the forest caving.

What was the fate of the TCB itself? Where did it fall after bouncing off the Earth? Can any clues be found? It is possible! - as Yordanishvili believes - although not very accurate. Taking into account the laws of mechanics, it is possible to predict the further flight of the TM and the possible place where the TCB is currently located in whole or in fragments. The scientist gives such clues: a line from the factories of Vanavara to the mouth of the Dubche or Voronovka rivers (tributaries of the Yenisei), the place: either branches of the Yenisei Mountains or in the taiga spaces between the Yenisei and Irtysh rivers... Let's note that the records and reports of the expedition from the 1950s and 1960s write about craters and tree outcrops in the areas of the western tributaries of the Yenisey - the Sym and Kiet' rivers. Their coordinates fit perfectly with an extension of the trajectory along which TM is believed to have flown toward Earth.

Commenting on the hypothesis of the Leningrad scientist, AN USSR correspondent member Prof. A. Abrikosov said:

...the concept of the meteorite «ricochet» on contact with the Earth makes sense, because the meteorite followed a tangent with the Earth and, after bouncing off it, fell into the taiga, where it rests to this day. This hypothesis not only explains a few question marks, but also finds its confirmation: there are post-impact formations at the sites of the alleged fall of TM remnants. This hypothesis is sure to revive the search for the TM, and perhaps there will come a time when it will be definitively found.

Corresponding with Yordanishvili's hypothesis is the view or version of Moscow astronomer V. Kovalev, published by WAGO in "Ziemla i Wsielennaja" No. 5/1989.

Starting from the fact that the forest howl at the epicenter of the explosion is not uniform, and has a complex geometry and internal heterogeneity, Kovalev suggests that there is no fact to counter the hypothesis that TCB was an ordinary stone meteorite... It was a real meteorite that exploded and disintegrated in the air. Its tremendous speed and great mass caused various strange phenomena in the atmosphere, including the cumulative, synergistic effect of shock waves from the explosion and ballistics. The forest blast zone is just such a place where these waves acted synergistically, i.e. overlapped. Only a study of this zone can give accurate data on the azimuth of the TM flight, the height of the explosion and where the meteorite debris fell... Yes, Kowal also talks about the ricochet effect and gives an example (sufficiently cursory and instructive at the same time) concerning the search for the Tsariev Meteorite, which fell on December 6, 1926 in the area of today's Volgograd.

Strangely enough, the fiery bolide was observed by thousands of witnesses and the trajectory of the fall of its remains was calculated based on their testimony. Unfortunately, an intensive search yielded nothing, and so it was forgotten after a while. It was not until 1979 that the meteorite was most simply found, and not where it was looked for, but as much as 200 kilometers away - at the extension of the trajectory of the flight... The story of the 157th in order of the discovery of the Russian meteorite Tsariev provides an altogether strong "pro" argument for the TM ricochet hypothesis.

The conclusion naproves itself: the TM should be looked for further and in a different place, and not where it was intensively sought by many researchers - at the epicenter of the aerial explosion.

This is evidenced, for example, by one of the latest publications on TM in the pages of Komsomolskaya Pravda on February 6, 1991. It says that taiga researcher Dr. V.I. Voronov, as a result of many years of searching, found at a distance of 150 km to the SE from the center of the air explosion - the so-called "Kulikovsky Caving" - another forest blowout with a diameter of about 20 km, which, he speculates, was found back in 1920 by the expedition of V. Shishkov. This latter howl may be related to TM, if we assume that it had already broken up into separate fragments during the flight.

In addition, in the autumn of 1990, this indomitable Voronov also found a huge funnel about 200 meters in diameter and 15-20 meters deep, densely covered with pine trees, at a distance of 100 km to the NW of the ""Kulikov's Caving". Some researchers believe that this funnel is a de facto astrobleme, which was carved by the "cosmic visitor of 1908" - he himself or parts of him. Tunguska Meteorite...

3.10. Electric explosion

In 1978, the academic journal "Astronomiczieskij Wiestnik" published an article by Prof. Dr . A. Nevsky, which later already in popular form appeared in "Tiechnikie Mołodioży" in 1978 - in number 12/1978. In it, the author considered the effect of an explosion under the influence of high-energy electric current, which is produced by large bolides during their flight through the atmospheres of planets.

The problem is that when - let's say - a large meteorite, moving at a significant speed, enters the Earth's atmosphere, as Nevsky's calculations indicate - a powerful potential flows between the meteor and the Earth. In such a case, in a fraction of a second, the kinetic energy of the meteorite calculated from a simple formula:

$E_k = \frac{1}{2}mv^2$

converts into the electrical energy of the discharge, which ultimately leads to the electro-explosion of the celestial body. Such an electro-explosion helps explain most of the observed TP.

The hypothesis under consideration shows that there are three types of shock wave sources - the explosive discharge of huge amounts of energy in the cylindrical space of the "fire pillar" generated a cylindrical shock wave, the vertical front of which spread horizontally to the ground surface, which became the cause of blowing the forest over a large area. However, it was not the only wave, as two others were created. The cause of the first was the explosive fragmentation of the meteorite's matter, while the second was an ordinary ballistic wave, which is generated by the passage of any body through the atmosphere at supersonic speed.

Such a course of events is confirmed by the stories of witnesses to the crash about the three independent explosions and the sound of the "artillery cannonade" that followed. It still needs to be said that the recognition of the fact of multi-channel electrical discharge clarifies many facts related to TM, including all the incomprehensible and mysterious ones. Without going into the details of Nevsky's hypothesis, I will only highlight the most important ones here:

The numerous individual channels of electro-explosion explain the existence of a vast space with a chaotic forest caving.

The action of electric attraction explains the facts of tossing yurts, trees, surface layers of soil into the air, as well as the formation of huge waves going up rivers - upstream.

The channels of the electrical explosions caused the formation of many small craters, which later became fogged with mud. This mud was not there before the explosion.

The impact of a strong electric charge on the ground caused strong heating of underground subterranean waters, resulting in boiling springs and geysers.

The strong pulses of electric current may have caused changes in the magnetic field and changes in the magnetization of rocks within a radius of 30-40 km from the epicenter of the TCB explosion.

The appearance of the unexplained to the end "white nights of the summer of 1908" can be explained by the electric glow of the ionospheric layers of the atmosphere due to the "cold" glow of ions - which is the process that occurs in the fluorescent...

The latter is confirmed by ground-based observations of phenomena accompanying the return to Earth of the US shuttle STS Discovery on November 16, 1984. The space shuttle then entered the atmosphere at a speed of Ma 16[48] and at an altitude of about 60,000 meters had the shape of a huge fireball with a wide braid or tail, but the most important thing is that it caused the upper layers of the atmosphere to glow.

Let's note another such moment... - there is a whole series of mysterious phenomena described by eyewitnesses of the TM fall, such as: "a humming swish", "a noise like the wings of a frightened bird", etc. Thus, these "acoustic effects" always involve so-called coronal electrical discharges!

Thus, we can assume that the physical processes guiding the electro-explosion of a meteorite are able to explain certain circumstances associated with the fall of large meteorite bodies, such as TM.

3.11. The mystery of the "Devil's Cemetery"

---

[48] Ma 16 = 5.28 km/s, assuming that 1 Ma = 0.33 km/s.

In the taiga of southern Angar, a few hundred kilometers from Vanavara, far from human settlements, there is a unique and mysterious place. The few residents of the area call the place "the glade of death" or "the devil's cemetery". I will cite a few testimonies here so that the Reader will have some idea of this "place of extermination."

Back in April 1940, a publication appeared in the Kezhm district newspaper "Sowieckoje Priangarie", saying that a hunter carrying the district agronomist before spring sowing to the village of Karamyshevo told him about the "devil's cemetery" that his grandfather had found near the animal path and promised to show this "clearing" to the agronomist. Here is what the newspaper wrote:

...a dark bald spot appeared next to an unremarkable mountain. The ground there was black and pulpy, but no vegetation grew there. On this bare ground they [placed] fresh green pine branches, and after a few moments they took them back. The green twigs turned brown, as if tanned by fire. The pine needles drooped at the lightest touch... Entering the edge of the glade, the people felt strange pains throughout their bodies...

Let me quote another story by S.N. Polyakov from the village of Karamyshevo:

My grandfather traveled 50 kilometers and came out to this glade. The moose he was tracking jumped out onto the flat part of the mountain ridge, and then jumped into the glade, where before my grandfather's eyes he fell and moments later burned. It was a very strong heat. Grandpa returned home immediately and told his family about everything.

The monthly magazine "Tiechnika Mołodioży" No . 8/1983 brought to light materials by M. Panov and V. Zhuravliev precisely on the subject of the "Devil's cemetery". In it Mikhail Panov relays a story heard before the war by a hunter who stayed at the so-called "devil's cemetery":

This is a large, very large, with a diameter of some 200 meters, a clearing that inspired fear. On the bare ground in places lay the corpses of animals, their bones, and even birds! The tree branches hanging over the clearing were charred, as if from a fire. The clearing was quite clear of any vegetation. The dogs that had been on it all for a few minutes had stopped eating and had become lethargic.

In addition to this, it should be added that the meat of animals that died in the glade took on a bright purple color.

Dr. Viktor Zhuravliev, who is a member of the Commission on Meteorites of the Siberian Branch of the AN of the USSR, confirms that there are no small number of independent accounts of the existence of a "place of doom" in the valley of the Kova River.

And here is a possible interpretation of this natural phenomenon and the origin of the "Chort cemetery" given by him:

At this location, a huge coal fire has formed deep in the Earth, which, due to the lack of air, produces large amounts of carbon monoxide - CO - or chad, extremely toxic to humans and animals. This gas is released right in this clearing. Animals without oxygen quickly die, and their tissues, due to a chemical reaction with this gas, turn a mottled-pink color.[49]

Well, yes, but the evaporation of lighter-than-air carbon monoxide is difficult to explain the peculiarities of the "devil's cemetery", as is the sharply defined boundaries of the lethal zone, and most importantly, the speed with which this zone kills living organisms - and most importantly, this whole " glade of death" is not located in a cleft in the terrain, but on the slope of a sloping sopka![50] The peculiarities of the "glade of doom" can be easily explained, some scientists say - if we assume that there is a source of electromagnetic radiation or a fast-variable magnetic field there. But what does TM have to do with it? It turns out that it does!

In the mid-1980s, in the newspaper "Komsomolec Uzbekistana", A. Simonov - a researcher at the NII Department of Physics at TGU and S. Simonov - a GMI employee of the Uzbek SSR[51] published their hypothesis about the origin of the TP. These scientists believe that:

...TM came from the south and flew north, flying magnetized more and more due to the «dynamo effect». Flight in the Earth's atmosphere caused heating and ionization of the air surrounding the meteorite body. Crossed by streams of ionized air, the magnetic field lines of force created electric and magnetic hydrodynamic (MHD) effects in its gaseous - actually plasmatic -

---

[49] In humans, there are pink precipitation spots due to the reaction of the oxygen-carrying blood component hemoglobin with carbon monoxide, resulting in carbo-oxyhemoglobin instead of oxyhemoglobin. The same is the case with light gas poisoning.

[50] Low volcanic cone.

[51] Uzbekistan today.

envelope, which had a weighty effect on the movement of the meteorite in our planet's atmosphere..

When TM flew into the lower and denser layers of the atmosphere, the air currents stripped it of its plasmatic «covering» and the meteorite, which retained a small fraction of its initial velocity, fell somewhere into the depths of the taiga of southern Priangaria, and the plasmid itself - consisting of a thicket of highly ionized air and electromagnetic fields, after breaking away from its «parent» - meteorite - became a huge ball lightning.

What was the further fate of the plasmid? The events of 1908 took place in a not-quite-ordinary place on Earth, as in the area of the East Siberian Magnetic Anomaly of planetary scale. «Magnetized» plasmid cloud began to move towards the pole of this anomaly. During its 350 km flight, the plasmid encountered the magnetic anomaly of a Paleo-volcano crater that was active millions of years ago. Its chimney entering deep into the ground - all the way into the ocean of magma in the asthenosphere - played the role of a «lightning rod» here, over which it discharged its electricity, causing the taiga trees to explode and cave...

This is, of course, only a hypothesis, but it offers hope for finding the meteorite, if it exists. Perhaps the TM may have "fallen out" down or to the side of the trajectory and its resting place can be traced by studying magnetic or other anomalies with unusual properties - such as gravitational.

In order to be sure of the correctness of his guesses, A. Simonov organized an expedition in 1986 to the Kova River region, where, according to his estimates, the meteorite should have fallen. His joy was endless when he heard stories of a "devil's cemetery" there, there could be no better confirmation! To find it, he questioned all the old men who stood in his way, and from their stories he put together a picture, and - unfortunately - it was a mosaic!!! neither this nor any other expedition managed to find the "devil's cemetery".[52]

A. and S. Simonov explained the peculiarities of the "death glade" this way:

...living beings are killed by rapidly varying magnetic fields. As biology teaches us, there is a certain tolerance interval of electric current flowing through the blood, beyond which it decomposes electrolytically. Animals that died in the «death glade» had viscera that were pink in color, indicating that capillary flow of blood increased just before death, and the latter occurred due to massive thrombocytosis. The concept of an alternating magnetic field in the «death glade» explains a great deal: the speed of death, the effect even on flying birds, etc..

---

[52] The case of the mysterious sites in Siberia was digged out at the end of the 20th century by the well-known Russian ufologist Dr. Valery Uvarov, who appeared in the pages of German and British ufological magazines. It was he who described a similar case of mysterious constructions in Yakutia, which turned out to be a nuclear training ground and cosmodrome built back in Soviet times, more precisely in the late 1950s in the basin of the Vilyu River. Today, there is a drop site for rocket boosters fired from the military cosmodrome in Pliesetsk near Arkhangelsk. The subject of these constructions was taken up in 2000 by another Russian - Dr. Valentin Psalomshchikov in the pages of the journal "Kalejdoskop NLO". Articles by both authors are available in the journals: "Nieznany Świat" and "Czas UFO".

And so the mysterious glade remains undiscovered. Prospectors process the data received and dream of new expeditions.

3.12. Was there a "black starflighter"?

In mid-1988, a whole host of central newspapers and popular science magazines published rehashes of an old version by scientist and SF writer Dr. Alexander Kazantsev about an extraterrestrial spacecraft that exploded in 1908 over the Tunguska taiga. What did this version say?

The TM explosion is a unique phenomenon - he writes - which so far remains incomprehensible in all senses of the word. There is no hypothesis today that comprehensively explains all the anomalies associated with this catastrophe. Among the many expeditions that almost every year ventured into the taiga, there was also one under the auspices of Dr. Sergei P. Korolov himself, who - note!!! - wanted to get his hands on a piece of a spaceship from Mars! And such a piece was really found! - 68 years after the explosion, 1,000 kilometers from its epicenter, on the banks of the Vashka River in the Komi Republic. And this in a place located on the trajectory of the TM... Two workers fishing near the village of Ertom found an unusual piece of metal weighing 1.5 kg on the riverbank. When they hit it against a stone, a sheaf of sparks ejaculated from it. This caught the interest of the people, who sent it to Moscow.

The unusual alloy contained 67% cerium [Ce], 10% lanthanum [La] - which was separated from admixtures of other lanthanides, something no one in the world has ever managed to do - and 8% niobium [Nb]. The find revealed 0.4% pure iron [Fe], with no oxides - which is exactly what the stainless column in Delhi and the... lunar soil! The age of the metallic shard varies between 30,000 - 100,000 years.

The shape of the shard indicated that it was part of a spherical or toroidal structure about 1.2 meters in diameter. The magnetic properties of the alloy were original: in different directions of the shard, they changed even more than 15 times. Everything spoke in favor of this - and the researchers themselves admitted it - that the alloy was an artificial origins. On the other hand - the fundamental question was not answered: where and in what apparatuses or engines are such details and alloys used? Therefore, a suggestion was put forward: perhaps it was part of the antigravity engine of an extraterrestrial civilization's spacecraft???...[53]

Next, Kazancev recalls the 1969 discovery by American astronomer Dr. James Bagby of 10-12 moons of Earth with strange trajectories. Such satellites could be easily spotted with astronomical observations. And indeed, unknown space objects were observed in 1947, 1952, 1956 and 1957[54], with as many as two objects being seen in 1956 and 1957. The last sighting in 1957 was actually by Dr. Bagby.

---

[53] In Polish literature, it has been called a "Vashkian radio artifact".
[54] In 1997, I proposed the designation NOO (UOO - Unknown Orbiting Object) - for this category of UFOs.

In his publication in the American journal «Icarus« Dr. Bagby claims that the first observations in 1947 and 1952 were of a single «parent» cosmic body, which broke apart on December 18, 1955, and now represents a «family» of Earth's moons with diameters ranging from 7 to 30 meters, moving in 6 different orbits. In March and April 1968, Dr. Bagby managed to photograph several of these quasi-moons. This fact, astronomers believe, confirmed the hypothesis of the existence of reconnaissance sputniks[55], although it was still too early for that. But the date of December 18, 1955, according to Kazantsev, perfectly matched an orbital flare observed by astronomers. What was it? Some kind of natural object? - But why wasn't it observed earlier? And if it was ruptured by some forces of Nature, by what? Probably, as Russian scientist Dr. S. Božich assumes, some extraterrestrial starship, previously orbiting the Earth, exploded.

This raises a fundamental question: and why, prior to 1955, did no one see this strange body in a telescope? However, Bagby himself claims that there were such observations, but this is not the most important thing at the moment. The object could have entered the blast point from a different - higher - orbit. If this puzzling body was a starship, it was black in color - perfectly black: its surface absorbed all the energy from the Cosmos, as our solar batteries of Mir stations and other artificial objects circling the Earth do, and this is why it could not be seen from our planet!

---

[55] This motif was used by the Ukrainian SF writer G. Gulia in his novel "Gianeja" (Kyiv 1968), in which he warned Humanity of the possibility of an invasion by the highly developed CNT, which just used invisible spacecraft and spy satellites.

- and therefore from Earth it was possible to see the remains of the stargazer once it showed its non-black side after the explosion...[56]

Kazantsev thinks this can be used to explain the events of almost a century ago:

In 1908, a large spacecraft that should not have descended toward the Earth's surface flew into Solar System space: its lander exploded over Tunguska [57]. The starship itself remained in orbit, and having lost communication with the lander, it waited for the crew to return, automatically correcting its orbit to avoid falling to Earth. However, it ran out of fuel, and the starship should inertly fall to the planet's surface. It can be assumed that in the programs of its computers was written in the prohibition of falling on an inhabited world, so the self-destruct systems worked and an explosion occurred...

Debris still orbiting the Earth in the future will explain many phenomena related to the Tunguska event.[58] They are something real and can be touched by hands. By getting their hands on them, cosmonauts would be able to study, among other things, their

---

[56] During my TATRA PROJECT, I managed to prove the existence of Unknown Flying Objects invisible to the human eye, which I called IUFO - Invisible UFOs, in Polish NNOLs.

[57] At the end of the 1990s, Eng. Miłosław Wilk from Warsaw published his vision of an alien spacecraft and lander in his book titled "Sieć Wilka" (Warsaw 1999).

[58] Unfortunately, they won't explain anything anymore, because, as Peter Krassa writes in his work entitled "Tunguska. "Tunguska, das rätselhafte Jahrhundertereignis" (Frankfurt/M - Berlin 1995, my translation) - the remains fell into the Earth's atmosphere and burned there in the 1990s...

chemical composition, which would perhaps coincide with that of the "Waskian find," as well as other things we can only dream of...[59]

The hypothesis is quite neat and acceptable, but how have scholars addressed it? Is it in any way credible?

The answers to these questions, it seems to me, are contained in a commentary by Prof. V. Bronstein, published in the journal "Ziemla i Wsieliennaja" No. 4/1989. Let me be brief - he savaged the author of the hypothesis. He writes as follows:

All these facts that A. Kazantsev cites in support of his arguments upon checking turned out to be fiction, fabrications. Take, for example, this information about the finding of a metal shard, which, according to Kazantsev, belonged to the remains of an interplanetary spacecraft. Which scientists and at which institutes conducted qualitative analyses of this shrapnel? Where did they publish the results of their research? It turns out that only in the newspaper «Socjalisticzieskaja Industria» in the issue of January 27, 1985[60], in an article by Anomalous Phenomena Commission member V. Fomienko, while nothing was published in the scientific press, and could not be... None of the directors of

---

[59] Reading Pietro Kolosimo's book - "Ombre sulle stelle" and Graham Birdsall's articles from the pages of "UFO Magazine" in 1998, we learn that Russian scientists proposed to the Americans a joint expedition to the remains of this stellar aircraft, but NASA refused them, wriggling - attention!!! - lack of funds for frivolous research! Arrogance, ignorance or just plain stupidity? Most likely, on the other hand, it was the most ordinary human fear of the Unknown?...

[60] In Poland, the first to report this information was the monthly magazine "Przyjaźń" No. 4/1985, followed by some national magazines, including the Bydgoszcz-based "Fakty".

the institutes to whom the fragment of this «cosmo-scrap» was allegedly handed over for examination confirmed this fact. Nor has it been confirmed that the analysis was done by employees of the institutes quite informally. To hand over for analysis to scientists this piece of «scrap» V. Fomienko refuses to do so...[61]

Prof. Bronsztejn goes on to comment on Bagby's discovery as follows:

...you can prolong the arguments about «Bagby's moons», but what does TM have to do with it? Bagby himself does not mention a word about it! According to him, the accompanying object entered the dense layers of the Earth's atmosphere and burned up... Among Russian scientists and researchers of the Cosmos there is no S. Božić. Perhaps such a figure exists, but has nothing to do with astronomy...[62] The sad example of this story shows us that there are people in our country who blow sensational and unsubstantiated news that has nothing to do with the achievements of Russian scientists. Not only that - there are also newspaper editors in our country who publish these sensations without any control...[63]

---

[61] And rightly so, for the artifacts submitted to official science that testify to the existence of aliens were quickly lost in unexplained circumstances or destroyed. The CToH's supporters claim that this is due to the activities of Freemasonry, which wants to hide the fact of the existence of aliens in order to extract maximum benefits for themselves. Either way, the destruction of such artifacts as the "Kysucké spheres" or the " Żabno meteorite", for example, have a chastening effect on!...

[62] Dr. Sergei Bozhich is not an astronomer, but an officer scientist, a rocket designer who works with the Aerospace Forces of the Russian Federation.

[63] Indeed, a strange opinion! In the USSR, no press, radio or television

What can be added to this? Only one thing: the i's has been dotted and the t's has been crossed, but the questions remain!...

3.13. Tunguska Meteorite and Gravity

In November 1989, the daily newspaper Kaliningrad Oblasti[64] „Majak" published in its pages an article signed by Dr . L. Anistratienko, who saw the connection between TM and... gravity. The author of the hypothesis claims that:

...as long as there is no key to solving the TM mystery... as long as scientific intuition is needed to help figure out the great number of forms and manifestations of the Tunguska problem.

Made with EMC [65] calculations allowed Anistratienko to conclude that the strange flight of TM and also of everything we know under the name of Unknown Flying Objects (I do not address this problem in this work) is due to our erroneous picture of the physical phenomenon of gravity.

Without getting into the detailed mathematical apparatus of the theory, let's get straight to the point: The Sun, the planets and their satellites, as well as all other cosmic bodies do not attract

---

information could be given without the approval of the censor from the GLAVLIT and the KGB, well, unless there was an interest in the party and the KGB... - therefore, no one in their right mind would admit to doing an analysis "under the counter"!...

[64] Kaliningrad Oblast today.

[65] EMC (EDM) which means electronic digital machines - today computers.

each other at all, but just the opposite - they repel each other! In other words: the Moon repels from the Earth, the Earth from the Sun, etc. - so that the Universe is constantly expanding, which has been proven experimentally and observationally.

As you can see from this, gravity is caused by a torrent of incoming radiation from the Cosmos, which consists of 90% protons and exerts pressure on everything, which we feel as gravity... Wandering through space at tremendous speeds and in different directions, protons penetrate virtually without any problems through hard material bodies, with some of them reacting with its protons and neutrons, transferring their energy to them.

The amount of these particles of cosmic radiation is equal in all directions - it is isotropic radiation - and all its pulses are aligned. However, when a cosmic body is "obscured" by another, the stream of particles will be shielded by it and become weaker. Such imbalances in the distribution of cosmic influence will cause these bodies to move closer to each other due to the forces of cosmic pressure from Earth to Moon and Moon to Earth. Therefore, Anistratienko argues, instead of the term "attraction" we should comprehend the "pushing" of the celestial bodies towards each other.

Further Anistratienko considers the TM problem from the position of his hypothesis on the nature of gravity, I will only give here the quintessence of his views on the matter.

More than 90 years ago, the eternal balance between Earth and one of its microsatellites was broken. The reason for this was the approach of three astronomical bodies: Earth, the mini-satellite and the incoming Halley's comet - a subject that will be further discussed in subsection 4.2. The approach of the meteorite-minisatellite to Earth remained in equilibrium and had no side effects, because the forces of inertia and cosmic pressure acting on the meteorite nullified each other. The system of bodies: Earth - TM was static. This changed when Halley's comet appeared on the horizon, upsetting this balance, and its repulsive force shot the TM minisatellite into the Earth's atmosphere. We know the rest.[66]

The testimony of witnesses who observed the TM fall west of the epicenter of its explosion can be used to support this hypothesis. These witnesses saw the TCB flying visibly upward - as if repelled from the Earth, which formed a fiery column... As you can see it clearly, Anistratenko's version cuts clearly from everything I have said here so far about the "cosmic ricochet" and TM's flight through Earth's atmosphere.

---

[66] Unfortunately - or perhaps fortunately - life has not confirmed Anistratenko's theory, because for all intents and purposes the Earth should be bombarded with meteorites, comets and other bits of cosmic material every time a comet or other celestial body approaches it, not to mention the fact that this hypothesis does not explain the peculiarities of the movement of comets in the Solar System! This hypothesis does not explain at all the origin and evolution of galaxies and other cosmological objects, much less "black holes", the existence of which is proof directly of the classical theory of gravity!

4. FACTS, THOUGHTS, CONCLUSIONS

4.1. The mysteries of the "Tunguska Miracle"

As long as scientists argued about what the TM actually represented, formulated their ever-new hypotheses in order to disprove them later - everything was fine. Meanwhile, some anomalous biological effects began to be observed at the site of the Tunguska event: a sharp increase in the number of mutations in trees and an increased growth of the forest biomass.

In 1976, an employee of the Institute of Cytology and Genetics of the SO AN of the USSR, Dr. V.A. Dragavtsev established that the number of mutations in Scots pine - Pinus silvestris - increased sharply in the TM flight zone, with the maximum of mutations observed at the epicenter of the presumed explosion. As is well known, mutations arise as a result of irradiation of genetic material with ionizing radiation, and in some cases it can also be chemical compounds[67] and electromagnetic disturbances.[68]

---

[67] One more thing that should be mentioned here is that rare earth elements - and their isotopes - are radioactive, which may have had a positive effect on plant growth and the occurrence of genetic mutations.

[68] Recently, the well-known Slovak ufologist Dr. Miloš Jesenský in 2001 announced a hypothesis that pandemic diseases such as AIDS, for example,

What was the cause of the mutation in the Tunguska event area is not known. Further research is needed.

There is also this version: at the TM explosion the ozone layer above the epicenter was severely damaged. Through the resulting "ozone hole", a cascade of strong ultraviolet radiation - so-called UVB and UVC - which is lethal, carcinogenic and mutagenic - entered the Earth's atmosphere, and thus could have caused changes in the genotype of pine trees and other trees.

Trying to tie the ultraviolent annual growth of pine trees to the ecological effects of the catastrophe: better illumination of the locality after the top of the forest fire or the knockdown of the forest by shock waves, the cessation of permafrost, the enrichment of the soil with mineral salts after the forest fire, etc. - does not explain everything. Nor has it been proven that the dust created after the TM explosion fertilized the soil to such an extent that it stimulated the growth of pine trees and other plants. According to specially conducted modeling studies, some micronutrients, especially rare earth elements such as lanthanum (La) and ytterbium (Yb), whose concentration in the 1908 soil and peat layers is significantly elevated, may have been responsible for this effect.[69] Let us also note that the area of occurrence of this lanthanum-iterbium spot coincides with the projection of the trajectory of the TCB on the taiga area...

---

were brought to Earth from the Moon by an American or Soviet probe that crashed in equatorial Africa, near Lake Victoria.

[69] There are mutagenic chemicals like dioxin that also create lethal mutations.

Isotope microanalysis further revealed that peat and soil samples taken from the TM explosion site also contained particles of bromine (Br), selenium (Se), arsenic (As), zinc (Zn), silver (Ag), iodine (I) and several other elements. Perhaps their presence in the soil stimulated rapid forest growth to replace the scorched taiga.

Russian scientists S. Golenetskiy, V. Stepanok and D. Murashev prepared a special fertilizer on the basis of soil studies from the Podkamennaya Tunguska region, which they then tried on the fields of the "Mir" kolkhoz in Tverskoy Oblast and the M. Kutuzov kolkhoz in Kaluga Oblast. The results of the experiment exceeded the wildest expectations! Thus, for example, potato yields increased by 43-47%, while the increase in the biomass of grasses and other experimental plants turned out to be 5-10 times greater than normal!

The question should be asked here: does this effect have anything to do with TM? There can be no unequivocal answer to it, because the whole problem lies in the fact that the whole Earth is sprinkled with cosmic or cometary dust every day. And so, counting slightly, 90 years after the TM explosion there will be exactly the same amount of this dust as before it... So this is not the way to go!

The conclusion imposes itself: the cosmic dust that is constantly falling into the atmosphere of the Earth has served as a stimulator of plant growth. And as long as our planet moves in its orbit piercing through the streams of dust and all the dust clouds that fall on its surface, isn't this the solution to the mystery of the emergence of pandemics of these or other diseases, fertile and infertile years, acceleration and deceleration of tree growth, etc.? At the same time, all of this is only conjecture and hypothesis.[70]

Let's go further... The explosion in the Evenk taiga - this is the clearest, but not the only episode of the complex whole of geophysical phenomena that were observed in 1908. They are very often underestimated - just such "luminous nights"... This phenomenon has become a "stumbling block" for omnipotent explanations of the nature of TCB.

Indeed - the luminosity of these nights cannot be explained by the mere scattering of the sun's rays on the particles of a meteorite sprayed in the air. The decrease in the intensity of this phenomenon after a few days allows us to believe that in this case a decisive role was played by ionization processes, the source of which was the deceleration by the Earth's atmosphere of a swarm of cosmic dust particles - a cloud - through which the Earth passed in a few days...

Other explanations for the phenomenon of "luminous nights" were submitted by Leningrad University researcher Dr. S. Nikolskij and E. Szulc, who, studying atmospheric opacity data in California in the early years of the 20th century, concluded that in 1908 an other cosmic body entered the Earth's atmosphere before the fall of TM - it was the Aleutian Meteorite. Its mass was about 100,000 tons, and it consisted of dust. The AM scattered in the

---

[70] Typical mutations of this kind are genetic changes in plants resulting from super-strong magnetic fields in so-called crop circles and pictograms. These mutations are manifold and their nature is not yet thoroughly investigated, due to the reluctance of the world of official science to study, among other things, UFOs and their interaction with the environment of our planet.

atmosphere a month and a half before the fall of TCB and caused the atmosphere to become cloudy - as well as glowing - before June 30, 1908. This is not an indisputable version, but it proves that even 90 years after the event, new facts can be found and an interesting new hypothesis can be made based on them...

And finally, the last thing - the nature of TM could be penetrated by studying not only the physical image of the explosion, but, above all, by studying the post-explosion remains - that would be it! This means looking for some object where these residues could have been found and "frozen" in 1908.

This, object turned out to be peat. It was examined in various ways and by various methods. The area of the disaster was combed literally meter by meter - about 15,000 square kilometers were searched. microscopic particles were examined, into which, logically, TM should have disintegrated. In the peats that were examined, it was possible to find 5 types of cosmic particles of interest - in this number silicate and iron-nickel particles.

As a result, an elevated amount of the heavy isotope of carbon - 14C - was found in silicate particles from the 1908 peat. This radioisotope appears in bodies subjected to strong cosmic radiation. It is an overt testimony that these silicon particles have an unequivocally and indisputably extraterrestrial origin. Calculated from the radioisotopic composition and distribution of the particles on the ground surface, the mass of TCB could be around 5,000,000 tons.

In 1980, diamond-graphite crystalline fusions of non-terrestrial origin were found in peat deposits in the "catastrophic" layer after special processing by researchers of the Institute of

Geochemistry and Mineral Physics of the AN USSR in Kiev. Such a thing is known to be formed exclusively at extreme pressures when explosions occur in kimberlite chimneys, or when space bodies hit each other or the Earth's surface. Since there were no explosions there in 1908, this would mean that an ordinary meteorite ripped through the taiga on June 30, 1908... - which does not mean that the TP problem ended with that! There are still many more mysteries! Analysis of photogrammetric maps of the vicinity of Podkamennaya Tunguska showed that there is a crater with a diameter of about 18 km near the crash site. It was always thought to be an old Mesozoic volcano 200 million years old. It turned out to be an astroblem! - a trace of a collision between the Earth and a meteorite 200 million years ago! Thus, these diamond-graphite fusions may come from that catastrophe... The shock waves of the Tunguska explosion may have "come up" these diamonds to the surface, as happens in such cases.[71] Therefore, it would be necessary to study this old astroblem first, which has not been done to this day!!!

In the early 1980s, American scientist Prof. Dr. R. Ganapathy - an expert on meteorites - conducted a study of the chemical composition of samples of Antarctic ice armor. He calculated that the snow that fell after the Tunguska event of 1908 should lie at a depth of about 10 m. According to his data, the ice from a depth of 10.15-11.05 m should contain snows from the year 1912±4

---

[71] Proof of the above are the mines of gold and other minerals in the Otago province of New Zealand, explored by Polish ufologist Prof. Dr. Eng. Jan Pająk, which were also "shaken" from the ground during the collision with the meteorite that formed the Tapanui astroblem in 1176.

years, and therefore from the years 1908-1916. Analysis of dust from this depth indicates that the amount of iridium (Ir) in the ice is six time higher than in other ice layers! Iridium, is an element rare on Earth, but rich in meteorites.[72] Ganapathy links this anomaly to the TP and estimates the mass of the TM at 7,000,000 tons, and the diameter at 160 meters.[73]

Analysis of metallic pellets from a 1908 peat layer excavated by a group of Russian scientists in the area of the Tunguska explosion also showed a 5 times higher iridium content than in the results obtained by Ganapathy! However, several circumstances must be kept in mind when evaluating these extremely interesting facts.

As I have already mentioned, in May 1908, a large iron-nickel meteorite flew apart in the Earth's atmosphere in the Aleutian archipelago region. The cloud of space dust scattered in the atmosphere and then fell in a vast space. The event may have significantly disturbed the background of cosmic dust particles and led to the appearance of anomalies in the chemical composition of soils dating back to 1908 and not related to TM on a whole series of points on the globe. In addition, geologists have discovered that certain types of volcanic aerosols, which are ejected by them from the Earth's great depths into the atmosphere, contain increased iridium levels!!!

---

[72] The prevalence of iridium on Earth is only 3 x 10-5 ppm, while its global reserves are only 950 tons.

[73] In this way, the mass of the asteroid that fell to Earth 65 million years ago creating the Chicxulub astroblem in Yucatan was also calculated, causing the zaurocyd.

To make things even more interesting, at a time not far from the fall of TM, a powerful eruption of the Xudach volcano was recorded in the same Aleutians. And also such a piece of information: data obtained from the study of layers from ice cores from near the South Pole from a depth indicating 1908 showed that there was no increased iridium content over the background, with the amount of iridium being much lower than that detected by Ganapathy!

And so the question of the remnants of the meteorite still remains open to this day. And this means that the picture of what we call TM today is not clear to this day.

4.2. Tunguska meteorite vs Halley's comet

People have been familiar with comets since ancient times. For millennia they have been observing them and for millennia they have been trying to explain their mysteries, but after one has been explained, another one appears and another one...

Our old acquaintance - comet P/Halley, which quite recently, in March 1986, for the thirtieth time in the memory of Mankind, arrived in the vicinity of our planet, is also no different. And it must be said that each of such randez-vous, apart from the magnificence of the spectacle, usually caused nothing but mindless fear.[74]

---

[74] This statement is untrue, as this fear was usually justified. Most likely, then - at the time of the passage of a bright comet near our planet - meteorites and

As you can see, for this, according to the Soviet scientist, physicist Dr. K. Pierebijnos in his article titled "Poputczik komety Galleja"[75] in the journal "Tiechnika Młodioży" No. 1,1984 - there should be some indications, real on a material basis. And they do exist: Pierebijnos cites a whole catalog of perfectly documented accounts of natural catastrophes from the annals of our civilization, which show a coincidence with the perihelion dates of the appearance of Halley's comet in the period between the years 1531-1910.

In addition, on the eve of Halley's comet's "cosmic visit", astronomers observe increased bolide activity, which was noticed as early as 1908 and was also observed in 1983-1985. Every now and then, news of the appearance of large bolides, several times more than usual, appeared in the specialized and daily press.

As Pierebijnos calculates, Halley's comet moves in its orbit not alone, but in the company of many other small crumbs of matter that are strung out over a large space.

As long as Halley's comet has been moving in its orbit for more than 100,000 years, the swarm of dust and particles has long since closed its elliptical track and is found along the entire length of its trajectory. There are comet debris of various sizes and

micrometeorites fell to Earth, as well as microorganisms contained in them that cause epi- and pandemics...

[75] Ad litteram, "Halley's Comet's traveling companion." In 1997 we had the opportunity to see the separation of such a "traveling companion" from the nucleus of comet P/Hale-Bopp, which caused, among other things, the suicide of members of the "Heaven's Gate" sect.

masses ranging from a fraction of a milligram to several hundred tons.

The decay products of Halley's Comet: stony and icy meteors, according to Pierebijnos, are of different consistencies. They range from rare to the most massive, which form a kind of "comet shockwave" whose "front" overtakes it by some 2 billion km - or 13.3 AU. The decay products form an elongated cloud moving along the comet's orbit. It has a width of 0.13 to 0.26 AU and a length of 0.8 to 1.2 AU - and there may be more than one. It is calculated that the diameter of meteorite bodies in such swarms can be up to several meters or more. Pierebijnos claims that the Earth met them between autumn 1983 and July 1984. All his earlier predictions came true accurately.[76]

Most important for us are the observations made during the fall of the Chulimsky (or Tomsk) Meteorite. On the evening of February 26, 1984, the flight of a brightly glowing celestial body with an orange-colored tail was observed in the sky of western Siberia. Having reached a tributary of the Obu River - the Chulym River - at an altitude of about 100 km above the Earth, the bolide flashed and exploded. In Tomsk, meanwhile, the following strange sound and visual effects were observed, underground tremors, light bulbs burned out in houses (!!!), and photo-elements fell out of electronic devices at the airport.

The astonishing thing about this whole story is that a visitor from Space without touching the ground of our planet caused an

---

[76] In 1986-1987, I had the opportunity to observe unusually brightly glowing silvery clouds over the Szczecin Coast and Greater Poland, which were related to the passage of Halley's comet near Earth in early 1986.

earthquake, which was confirmed by all the surrounding seismic stations. The thing is, there hasn't been a single underground quake there in 10 years![77] And on that day, February 26, as many as 8 stations recorded ground shaking! The TNT equivalent of the energy of this earthquake was about 3 kt TNT, while the energy of the explosion of the bolide in the atmosphere was estimated at more than 11 kt TNT.[78] The air wave generated by the explosion was felt within a 150-kilometer radius of the blast's epicenter as a rumble of lightning.[79]

The expedition of the Institute of Geology and Geography of the Siberian Branch of the AN USSR, which was sent to the taiga in the summer of 1984, was not able to find the remains of the meteorite. And one more interesting circumstance: well, the trajectory of CM perfectly copied the trajectory of TM!!! This fact, unexplained by anyone, has given rise to a lot of unexpected speculation... Well, if we are to take seriously the enunciations of Dr. Pierebijnos, then the answer follows by itself: both TM and CM turn out to be representatives of "the entourage of Her Majesty Halley's Comet", which at each approach to the Sun bombards the Earth with its debris![80]

---

[77] The area is a pseismic area, i.e. earthquakes are extremely rare there.

[78] That is, about as many as the first A-bombs tested by the Americans in New Mexico and Japan.

[79] Perhaps, it was just an attempt by a Soviet or Chinese ICBM, which got out of control and was destroyed either on command from Earth or as a result of an OPB weapon. Such things happened more than once in the USSR.

[80] Perhaps a larger fragment of Halley's comet (the so-called Planetoid A) sent the legendary land of Atlantis to the bottom of the Atlantic, which may have happened about 12,000 years ago.

***

A meteorite, a bolide, a comet, a cold fragment of a comet's head, a piece of antimatter, a laser pulse from the 61 Cygni star planet, a plasmid - that is, a piece of the Sun, an alien spacecraft, a natural gas leak and even... a black hole!... More than a hundred hypotheses have been linked to the mysterious explosion that shook the Siberian taiga over Podkamennaya Tunguska on the morning of June 30, 1908.

115 years have passed since that explosion. To this day, rich factual material has been collected, many theoretical models have been constructed and analyzed in the fire of many interesting experiments.

What is being done today to solve the mystery of TM? In what direction is the search going? The collection of materials is underway, and at the same time a great deal of work is being done to systematize what has been collected in previous decades. So, what should be done...? It would be appropriate here to recall a statement made by ANM[81] USSR's academician Prof. N. Vasiliev in September 1986 to a correspondent of "Komsomolskaya Pravda":

...unfortunately, the overall theory of the Tunguska phenomenon is to this day unexplained and not even formulated. I think that the solution will be found by way of modification of the cometary version. However, I will tell you something - unexpected twists in this matter are possible...

---

[81] Academy of Medical Sciences of the USSR.

Let's look at some facts: back in 1971, a scientific employee of the KM AN USSR I. Zotkin published an article entitled "Tunguska meteorites fall every year," in which he writes:

...the Earth's surface can only be reached by dense, massive meteorites with a relatively low velocity relative to the Earth - Vg ≤ 20 km/s - while the entry corridor into the atmosphere is remarkably narrow.

The corridor of entry into the atmosphere runs at a slight angle, and so, for example, for the Soviet spacecraft of the Probe series this angle was about 17o±2. In the case of an angle of less than 150, the spacecraft is reflected from the atmosphere and returns to Space, in the case of greater than 190 - burn up in the upper layers of the atmosphere. When the thing involves a meteor, such a meteor reflected from the upper layers of the atmosphere becomes a bolide, while one entering the atmosphere becomes a meteorite. Perhaps - as suggested by V. Khokhriakov - TM entered the Earth's atmosphere at a slight angle and became a bolide - as a result, there is no astrobleme and no material traces of its passage other than the uproar of the forest caused by the shock waves of the ballistic blast...

Such a bolide could have been electrically charged, and if A. Nevsky is right, then a meteor with a diameter of 300 m and a speed of 15 km/s caused the conversion of kinetic energy into electrical energy already at an altitude of 25 km. It should be added that this change is in the nature of a very strong explosion.

An objective and reliable approach to Nevsky's theory allows us to conclude that we are talking about a real physical phenomenon, and that with its help the entire course of the TP can be explained.

Nevsky's hypothesis does not interfere with others, and fits perfectly with most scientific versions - except the most extravagant ones - about the origin and nature of the TM.

5. POSTSCRIPT

Well, and we finished the story of TM, its mysteries and puzzles. It's time for a conclusion. What actually happened in the Siberian taiga on the morning of June 30, 1908?

Today we can only sketch such a picture of the whole phenomenon: a certain cosmic body - most likely belonging to Halley's comet - descended from its heliocentric orbit and at a speed of tens of kilometers per second, at an angle of between 10-20° - or even 30° - entered the Earth's atmosphere from the eastern or even southeastern direction. At an altitude of 30-50 kilometers above the Earth, it fragmented or shattered, and the debris flew apart in various directions. The main part of the TM entered the dense layers of the atmosphere and accumulated a significant electrical charge, which then discharged between it and the Earth's surface. In a short time, the bolide's kinetic energy transformed into electrical energy, which happened at an altitude of 5-10 km. This electric explosion manifested itself with many unique physical effects.

What did the space visitor consist of? - This has not been determined so far. Yes, we have a proposal that the TM consisted of light compounds of carbon and hydrogen, as well as silicon, aluminum, zinc, etc. It was not a meteor in the broad sense, but a fragment of the nucleus of Halley's comet, which arrived in the perimeter of the Earth's orbit to find itself at the solar point of the orbit on April 20, 1910.

When analyzing the event of June 30, 1908, we use the words: probably, perhaps, it seems, etc. all the time. This was necessary when showing one hypothesis or another. And so the TP problem seems to have been solved with the help of mathematical calculations that explain the entire physical basis of the phenomena occurring at the explosion...

And one more event and one more circumstance related to the fall to Earth of cosmic bodies similar to the TP. It is known that cosmic bodies with diameters not exceeding 1 km are periodically approaching our planet. They may belong to the Asteroid Belt (asteroids), as well as to comets passing near Earth. Astronomers have calculated that the probable collision of Earth with such an asteroid is very rare - once every 150,000 years.

In the history of our planet there are recorded plural traces of such catastrophes, and the time since the last one causes us a feeling of anxiety - but from this we do not feel worse at all, and safer we will not be at all...

Modern developments in science and technology make it possible to predict and possibly prevent such collisions, and to do so with the help of what was prepared for the doom of all Mankind. And so, for example, the American physicist of Jewish-Hungarian origin, Professor Dr. Edward Teller, proposed the use of hydrogen warheads to destroy asteroids. In his speech at George Washington University in 1989, this scientist also mentioned the catastrophic consequences of a TM drop and pointed out the necessity of destroying such celestial bodies before they reach Earth.

According to Teller, the explosion of a thermonuclear charge could fragment a celestial body into tiny fragments that would present no danger with themselves.[82] As a first practical step in this direction, Teller proposed to conduct experiments with the destruction of meteorites or comet companions that pass in close proximity to our planet...[83]

And finally... - analysis of the situation created by the solution of the TM problem and submitted in this work, does not at all pretend to be considered the final word on the matter. Perhaps new facts will come to light and a revision of all previous views on the origin and nature of TCB will be needed.[84]

---

[82] This finding is highly problematic, as meteorite dust can cause significant atmospheric turbidity, with a consequent change in the solar constant and lowering of the Earth's surface temperature, heavy rains and floods, as well as other related disasters.

[83] There are two defense programs, PROJECT ICARUS and PROJECT ORION, which involve the massive use of thermonuclear weapons against asteroids like 4179 Toutatis, which will approach Earth at a distance of 0.01 AU (passed safely) on September 29, 2004, and collide with our planet on August 14, 2126!

[84] Not long ago, Giżycko astronomer Roman Rzepka, in his article titled "Czarne <<słupy kurzu>> i niezwykłe kamienie" (Black <<dust pillars>> and unusual stones) in "Nieznany Świat" No. 5/2000 writes that he found in 1997 in the vicinity of Giżycko , a dozen kilometers north of the city, strange meteorites, which, according to local legends, fell there about a hundred years ago, so somewhere around 1908... Their chemical composition shows similarity to meteorites from outside the solar system, and therefore from outside the Oort Cloud! Analysis has shown conclusively that these meteorites do not contain even a trace of nickel, like those from the Solar

System. The "pillars of black dust" mentioned in the title of the article accompanied the fall of these meteorites. Of course, official science did not deign to take a position on the matter in question!!!... - which is a pity, because a thorough study of these stones could solve one of the biggest mysteries of the century... These stones look inconspicuous - they are grayish-black, and on the breakthroughs shine balls of metal - meteoritic iron. Perhaps this is indeed a "warm" trace of the fact that TM was actually a cosmic body that moved at hyperbolic speed - i.e. with Vg > VIV or even Vg >> VIV - which in itself is a scientific super-sensation!!!

PART II
OTHER VIEWS, NEW SUGGESTIONS

6. P. I. Privalov – LIST OF HYPOTHESES ABOUT THE TUNGUSKA BOLIDE

In composing this catalog, the following were included: 390 articles, about 180 papers, more than 550 popular science reports, columns, notes; 60 novels, short stories and poetic and dramatic works; 10 monographs; 5 movies , radio and TV broadcasts, painting and graphic works, epistolary, archival and other materials. Musical works dedicated to the phenomenon under consideration do not yet exist.

LIST OF HYPOTHESES ABOUT THE TUNGUSKA BOLIDE

As of 01.01.1969[85]

1. Atomic explosion of interplanetary ship arriving from Mars. (1946)

2. Landing of a spacecraft that decelerated using rocket engines. (1950)

---

[85] Translated from Russian. - **Bolesław Baranowski**.

3. Successful launch of a spacecraft after a brief visit to Earth. (1951)

4. Arrival of a spacecraft from Venus. (1958)

5. A spacecraft that contained copper conductors and semiconductors. (1958)

6. Automatic spy apparatus from Venus. [86] (1959)

7. A rocket with doors and windows, which determined the shape of the shock wave. (1960)

8. Nuclear explosion of unknown cause. (1960)

9. UFOs fall, land or disintegrate. (1961)

10. Laser beam projected from star planet 61 Cygni. (1964)

11. The spacecraft that transported the Yeti to Earth. (1965)

12. Cosmolote-contromote.[87] (1965)

13. Collision of two or more spacecraft, see 61. (1966)

14. Spacecraft maneuvered over Earth and malfunctioned. (1967)

15. The collapse of antimeteorite. (1947)

16. Annihilation of antimatter mass in the atmosphere. (1958)

---

[86] This hypothesis was first presented by Stanislaw Lem in his novel "The Astronauts" written in 1953, and the same applies to the A-6 hypothesis, for Lem clearly wrote about the TM spy mission, which was to precede the Venusians' invasion of Earth after murdering the Earthlings with the help of a radioactive cloud emitted toward our planet.

[87] See A. Strugatsky, B. Strugatsky - "Monday Begins on Saturday", where the theory of countermotion (moving backward in time), continuous and discontinuous, is explained in an understandable way.

17. An explosion of the kind that destroyed the planet Phaeton. (1959)

18. Annihilation of antimeteorite, resulting in an increase in the amount of radioactive carbon C-14. (1965)

19. The Tunguska explosion as a statistical phenomenon with a probability of 1/7. (1966)

20. A piece of substance from the so-called white dwarf. (1966)

21. Ordinary meteorite + antimatter satellite. (1968)

22. Transformation of time, matter or space into energy. (XX)

23. The end of the world. (1908)

24. The coming of the Antichrist. (1908)

25. Descent from heaven of the god Agda (Ogda). (1908)

26. Flight of the Gorinich dragon. (1908)

27. A repeat of the Sodom and Gomorrah destruction. (1950)

28. A burst of ball lightning, or perhaps even several. (1908)

29. Earthquake caused a jolt in the air. (1908)

30. The beginning of the war with Japan - artillery cannonade. (1908)

31. Hurricane, tornado and forest fire. (1928)

32. Accident at artificial diamond factory. (1958)

33. Explosion of simulid and mosquito cloud with a volume of 5 km^3. (1960)

34. Electrical discharge between ionosphere and Earth caused by meteorite. (1962)

35. Generation of a lightning mixture by a flared meteorite in the permafrost. (1962)

36. Cataclysm of unknown nature in the antipodes. (1964)

37. Natural gas explosion from lightning strike. (1964)

38. Natural gas explosion from meteorite impact. (1968)

39. Disintegration of a giant aerolith over Kezhma. (1908)

40. Fall of a giant meteorite in the Podkamennaya Tunguska basin. (1922)

41. Meteorite disintegrated in the air and caused a shock wave. (1925)

42. Meteorite slammed into Earth in a stream of debris and gases. (1927)

43. Meteorite ricocheted off Earth's surface. (1929)

44. Earth collided with a dense cloud of cosmic dust, see 52. (1932)

45. Iron-nickel meteorite fell as shrapnel into a swamp. (1939)

46. The meteorite formed a crater that flooded a swamp. (1949)

47. Meteorite may have been made of ice. (1958)

48. The crash was caused by the ballistic wave of a passing meteor (bolide). (1958)

49. Stone meteor shower caused karst in permafrost. (1959)

50. The ballistic wave was caused by a meteorite that vaporized just above the ground. (1959)

51. It was a thermal explosion of an icy meteorite. (1960)

52. TM is the density of space dust. (1962)

53. The meteorite fragmented under the pressure of the air - see 75. (1964)

54. A bright bolide flew over Denmark or elsewhere. (1908)

55. Meteorite fell near Filimonov near Kansk. (1908)

56. The meteorite fell in the Kiet' (Kieć) River basin. (1948)

57. The meteorite ricocheted off in a northerly direction. (1958)

58. Iron powder meteorite burned up in the air. (1958)

59. Meteorite fell near Churgin Creek. (1959)

60. Electrostatic charge knocked down taiga. (1959)

61. Two meteorites collided in the air. (1959)

62. The meteorite broke into pieces that collided in the air. (1959)

63. The meteorite was small and the forest in the area of the fall was impermanent. (1960)

64. Meteorite fell in Lower Tunguska region. (1960)

65. The meteorite was carbon and burned to the ground. (1966)

66. Meteorite was torn apart by thermal stresses. (1967)

67. A comet or planet fell over Angara. (1908)

68. Comet P/Pons-Winncecke associated with the Bootyd swarm has fallen. (1926)

69. Earth collided with a dust-tail comet. (1934)

70. Comet P/Encke has fallen. (1958)

71. All indications are that it was a comet. (1960)

72. Chemical explosion of free radicals in comet. (1960)

73. Thermal explosion in the nucleus of a comet. (1960)

74. It was the same comet that destroyed Atlantis.[88] (1963)

75. Mechanical explosion of comet nucleus. (1964)

76. Comet 1874 II flew through the atmosphere. (1965)

77. Dissociation of water in a comet and explosion of the resulting lightning mixture. (1966)

78. Ice meteorite dissociated, burned and then a thermonuclear fusion happened. (1961)

79. Starship disguised as a comet. (1963)

80. Antimatter comet exploded in the atmosphere. (1965)

The article from which the above list was quoted entitled "Hypotheses related to the fall of the Tunguska Meteorite" was published in the magazine "Priroda" No. 5/1969. In Poland it was published in the SF almanac "Kroki w Nieznane" vol. 2, Warsaw 1971. so far is the only in the countries of Europe list of hypotheses on the nature and origin of the Tunguska Phenomenon.

---

[88] See also L. Zajdler - "Atlantis", Warsaw 1980.

7. M. Jesenský & R. Leśniakiewicz - HYPOTHESIS #81: AN ANCIENT NUCLEAR WARHEAD?

Only in 1983, the dean and one of the "popes" of Polish ufology, editor Lucjan Znicz-Sawicki, in his work entitled "Visitors from the Cosmos: Alien Traces" - which is part of a peculiar bible for Polish ufologists - commented on this list and added several other versions of the course of TP events, however, the above 80 hypotheses constitute what can be called the CANON OF HIPOTHESES ABOUT THE ORIGIN AND NATURE OF THE TUNGUSKA PHENOMENON, which we propose to include permanently in ufology. However, something can be added to this CANON, because science is moving forward and new facts are constantly being revealed that shed new light on the old problem of the origin of the TP. Our hypothesis No. 81 begins like a fairy tale...

It was a long, long time ago... - begins like a fairy tale, but by no means it was not a fairy tale, because it could have been, and in all probability this is how events unfolded. And how, we will tell the Reader shortly...

About 12-15 thousand years ago, there was a magnificent and developed Super-Civilization of Science and Technology on Earth. This SCST had at least 100,000 - 1 million years of development behind it, so it was older than ours and much more technically advanced than ours. It reached the nearest planets, and its forposts may have stood on the moons of the giant planets and Pluto... Evidence of this are various strange formations on the Moon and Mars: groups of pyramids, Martian Face, Tower, Castle, Spire, etc. There is a lot of it. On Earth, too, traces of it remain: pyramids and other megalithic structures, as well as those intangible traces in human memory in the form of legends, fables and religions. In the form of beliefs that made our ancestors carry multi-ton boulders, process them with incredible precision and erect monuments that remind us of the splendor of the fallen Supercivilization...

Because this SCST has fallen!

How it happened? that we do not know exactly, and what our ancestors have passed down to us does not allow us to form any coherent picture of the Great Conflict of a hundred and twenty centuries ago, because that is how we estimate the time of the Great Fall. The first (and perhaps not the last in the history of Humanity)!...

Most likely, there were sharp divisions in the bosom of this SCST that were not overcome by reasonable bargaining and negotiation - someone let his nerves go, someone reached for a gun. And once it was used, it was impossible to stop the bloodshed - what a familiar picture from Yugoslavia, Timor, Rwanda, Chechnya, Ulster, Ukraine and other hotspots of the world!

Negotiations broke down and Weapons of Mass Destruction (WMD) were used. What served the people became an instrument of murder and retaliation. The war raged on land, sea in the air and in space. Its results can still be seen today: the planet

Phaethon between Mars and Jupiter was milled into the crumbs that today form the Asteroid Belt; Mars was all annealed and then frozen almost to the cosmic temperature of the surrounding vacuum. On Venus, the warring parties led to a massive greenhouse effect, resulting in it being covered in lava and its atmosphere composed of carbon dioxide and sulfuric acid... The Moon was also insulted, on which now haunt - how improbably predicted (or only???) by Jerzy Żuławski in the early 20th century - corpse cities with soaring minarets towering 5-15 km above the lunar ground! Who put them there? Who destroyed them?

Not aliens, but humans. Humans and their machines, because it was a civilization of machines and much more perfect than ours. We fear that Humanity is once again driving itself into a dead end from which it may have no way out...

Or maybe it was different? Maybe this SCST of ours was not as evil and bloodthirsty as we have portrayed it here? Perhaps, during the reign of this Atlantis Supercivilization, the Earth resembled the Garden of Eden, where the Golden Age reigned? Everything that lived on Earth served Man, who protected and cared for the planet entrusted to him. Perhaps it was indeed Utopia - Dreamtime - as the Aborigines called this period, when Man could walk from Europe to Australia and from Australia to America with his bare feet without fear of snapping them on sharp stones or bushes... But happiness is not a permanent state if one does not take care of one's own safety. Our SCST has come face to face with an external threat. Here were aliens heading toward the Solar System, who had a craving for the five biogenic planets swimming in the solar ecosphere...

Who were the aggressors?

We once assumed that they might have been space apatricians - exiles from their homeworld, and the reason for the exile was the unfavorable conditions on the home planet (or planets): dimming of the native star, transformation into Nova or Supernova, a cosmic collision with another planet or a jet impact... - one does not know, and the possibilities are many. Imagine beings living with the hope that someday they will find a world where their civilization will be reborn and blossom again. They have been flying for hundreds or perhaps thousands of years, and all of a sudden a Solar System with Venus, Earth, Moon, Mars and Phaethon, all habitable, comes in their way. Unfortunately, they are already inhabited by a rational race of beings standing at a slightly different scientific and technological level. What then to do? There is no way out - to master these planets, of course! But they are already inhabited!

"We have no choice," the Beings decide, "it's either them or us. There is no third way out! We are tired of wandering around the Cosmos!"

"We attack the Earthlings!" the decision was made.

As a result of this decision, a terrible conflict occurred, as a result of which both civilizations collapsed! Life survived only on Earth, and even this only in a dwindling and rachitic form... Aliens and Mankind went back hundreds of thousands of years in development. All the achievements went into oblivion and rubble. When the smoke cleared, then everyone realized that it was necessary to start all over again. From scratch. And they started. From this was born our civilization...

What does TM have to do with all this?

A lot, because we assume that the SCST had everything that we already have plus some improved systems of the type of our SDI, ABM or MND - only that they were more technically advanced. These systems took part in the Conflict, but after the destruction of the coordination and command dispatch centers on Earth and other planets, there remained in space some unused combat satellites and "killer" satellites designed to destroy those in orbits around Earth or around planets. And they orbited for thousands of years around the Earth from time to time making minor adjustments to their orbit so as not to fall on it.

Such a state lasted for some time. After the fuel supply ran out, these satellites slowly succumbed to Earth's gravity, and from time to time one of them fell to our planet, and then a hell of a lot of A, B, C, H and N weapons were released, and maybe even D?[89] It was thanks to this that Humanity was plagued by the most terrible diseases, unexplained to this day epi- and pandemics, epi- and panzootics, incredible explosions and subsequent diseases, as vividly resembling radiation sickness, suffocating, poisonous fogs and scorching rains... The destruction of Sodom and Gomorrah could have been triggered not only by ancient nuclear warheads, but by ordinary napalm or phosphorus-celluloid incendiary plates - such fiery rains are well remembered by residents of Tokyo, Hanoi, villages in Afghanistan or Chechnya. A list of these God's tributes up to the 18th century was cited by Miloš in his excellent work titled "Bohové atomových vàlek" (Ústi nad Labem, 1998) and we will not cite it here.

---

[89] A = atomic weapons, B = biological, C = chemical , D = disintegration (from antimatter), N = neutron, H = thermonuclear, etc...

So what was TM?

In light of what we have said above, we can confidently assume that the TCB was nothing more than a multi-warhead rocket - the MIRV - that fell from Space to Earth in the Podkamennaya Tunguska region, and de facto exploded in mid-air - what's more - before it happened, it was moving through the air just like a self-steering Cruise or Tomahawk jet missile. What's more - this missile split tens of kilometers in front of the target into 2-5 fragments, which hit the target together or separately, attacking from several directions! Hence the three tree uproars and five explosion epicenters, hence the discrepancies in witness accounts, and hence, finally, all those thunder rumbles of exploding thermonuclear warheads. Hence all those geophysical phenomena, how they fit with the theory of the Kazantsev cosmolote explosion! Because it was a spaceplane, only that it did not carry a living or even automatic crew, but death and annihilation... Only that on Earth there was no longer a target to be destroyed...

Wasn't there?...

Or maybe the target was just an old volcanic chimney in the Lower Tunguska basin? If such a multi-headed missile had hit an old volcanic chimney, a series of five or maybe even more explosions with a combined power of 10-15 Mt TNT could have awakened the dormant volcano... How? - Very simply: the first explosion would turn 50-100 meters of ground, permafrost and rock into steam, the second and subsequent warhead hitting the same place would tear off further hundreds of meters of rock up to the magma reservoir... Stach to think what would happen to half the continent! The terrible terremoto would wreak havoc on half of Asia and all the volcanoes of Kamchatka and the Caucasus would be activated, not to mention the Tyan-Shan and Altai. Terrible environmental weapons that not even Supercivilization could face...

We may be wrong, but there are too many indications that this is what once happened. Legends and myths about the Great Conflict of the Gods are known on all continents and are told by all peoples: from the Aborigines and Albanians to the Zulus. The earth bears traces of Cyclopean construction, which even our civilization is unable to reconstruct, because stone - the most durable of all building materials known in Nature - was used for it, and we are unable to repeat the feat of our ancestors, and erect at least one stone pyramid on the model of the pyramid of at least Mycerinos... And for this nothing will help books that are critical in intent, but in fact dilute and obscure the matter, being a bunch of over-intellectualized gibberish, written by various "anti-Daeniken" or similar buffoons calling themselves in simple naivety "scholars", without panache and a shred of elementary imagination, because all these - bad - "treatises" or "critiques" are written on the principle: "negate whatever you can - and if you can't, laugh at it or ignore it altogether!". And that's what's most pathetic - because these "explainers" and "critics" come up with imprudent hypotheses of the kind served to us by Prof. Anistratienko, Bronstein and their ilk, in order to eclipse the clear picture of what was before our civilization came into being...

We believe that hypothesis No. 81 defends itself quite well, and there is enough evidence to support it - it is enough to take a good look around and think, although, on the other hand, we realize that in our devolved and totally stupefied by the sick educational system society with thinking is generally difficult - to put it mildly. We don't have time to look around, and to think, it's better not to talk at all. Following the speeches of some politicians or the actions of some scholars - most recently, Prof. Jan Ostrowski of Wawel Castle "shone" with his stupidity, who began to fight the Wawel Earth Chakra - I am increasingly convinced that blindness, envy and devotion go with the better in them with superstition, which they bombastically call "modern science." The other "scientist" who has recently made a lovely fool of himself is Prof. Dr. Janusz Gil, who stated that modern physics has already ended with the General and Special Theory of Relativity and all the rest are just cosmetic additions and nothing more. Hmmm... - well, what do we think - all Nobel Prize winners in physics after 1916 should give back their Nobel Prizes, as according to Prof. Gil - they did not discover anything revolutionary, but only made appendixes... Such foolishness this "modern science" scored even more, only that they are not talked about, because they are scrupulously hidden by their authors...

The evidence is there and not infrequently falls from the sky.[90] It is only necessary to look for them in the works of such authors

---

[90] The photo presented in the Gazeta Krakowska shows Theodore Salomons of a farm near the city of Worcester (150 km from Cape Town, South Africa) sitting in a field next to a metal ball that fell on directly from the sky. A second similar sphere fell 50 km from Cape Town. They were white-hot at the time of their fall. Astronomers believe they are parts of the Earth's artificial satellites that fell in the form of this "space junk." Other sources claim they are the remains of a booster of some spacecraft. Also in July 2023, a fragment of the booster of an Indian rocket launched in 2010 fell on an Australian beach.

as, among others: Aleksander Mora, Arnold Mostowicz, Lucjan Znicz-Sawicki, Andrzej Donimirski, Aleksander Grobicki - just to mention Polish authors here. They can also be found in ghastly garbages of the kind of "Back to Earth" read à rebours: one must look about to see what these authors "lightweight critics" did not write! Because the authors of this garbage in the fervor of huffing and puffing at opponents also dropped a bricks, and how cute! But criticism of this rubbish is beyond the scope of this paper, and we will spare the Reader to cite the list of fluffs of these people who consider themselves "real scientists"...

Hypothesis No. 81 ranks in the list of P. I. Privalov in the group of hypotheses A.

8. R. Leśniakiewicz - TM Z KOSMOSU

Let me return once again to the question posed at the beginning - What was TM? Several hypotheses have occurred to me in this matter, which preceded in time the hypothesis of the Great God-Astronaut Conflict, and the first two - I label them here hypotheses 82 and 83 - I formulated back in the 1980s, when I was beginning to be interested in ufology and paleocontacts in earnest. The first one assumes that we were then dealing with some kind of energy device that literally fell on our heads on that fateful day of June 30, 1908, while the second one says that we were dealing with a reconnaissance apparatus from another star system that crashed in Earth's atmosphere. These are modifications of the hypotheses marked in the "Canon..." under the headings A-14 and G-79 so let's start with the former:

8.1. Hypothesis #82: An energy device from many, many centuries ago?

Let's assume that this assumed SCST in hypothesis No. 81 de facto existed, and that for some unknown reason it was annihilated. This supercivilization, of course, conducted extensive research into the Cosmos and the Solar System. Let's say that there is a true theory about the existence of "traveling companions" of comets - and it's true, because we saw such a traveling companion that separated from the nucleus of comet P/Hale-Bopp - and that there was an Earth observation and research station on one of them, which circled the Sun once every 76.3 years along with comet P/Halley...

After the Conflict, this station was abandoned and its equipment was shut down and secured. And so the station orbited with the entourage of Halley's comet, from the Sun to Pluto - and thus all the way through the Solar System! If I had to decide where to place such a research station of the System, I would also place it precisely on such a celestial body passing through it! How much scientific data can be collected during such a trip! Benefits alone at minimal cost.

Of course, the station's power equipment had to be efficient, because solar energy could be used only up to the perimeter of Mars' orbit, and further on some other source of energy had to be used, and indeed - hydrogen from the hydrogen chamber of the comet's head, or even from the "dirty snow" that makes up its nucleus, was used. Hydrogen is an ideal fuel for thermonuclear reactors. Such a station must have contained a lot of equipment working on the basis of semiconductors and superconductors - hence in its mass were to be found such elements as silicon, selenium, germanium, yttrium, rhenium, lanthanum or cerium... The remains of one of its devices were found in the 1980s on the banks of the Vashka River in the Komi Republic.

In 1908, the station entered the Earth's atmosphere due to the perturbing influence of Jupiter, Saturn and the Sun. The effect of this event was one we remember from descriptions of TM's fall.

The explosion that sprayed the space station into the atmosphere was a "pure" thermonuclear explosion. There wasn't much left of the station, as it was torn into dust by the thermonuclear explosion, and within a few milliseconds it turned into a plasma cloud that also exploded in the lower layers of the atmosphere - and let's not forget that it must have been moving at the speed of Halley's comet - exactly the same speed - and that's tens of kilometers per second... Was this the body that flew through the field of view of Earth's telescopes and telescopes shortly before the fateful day of June 30, 1908?

I wonder if the station looked like our space stations of today, such as Salut, Skylab, Mir or MSK/ISS? Not likely, because being exposed to a continuous bombardment of cometary matter crumbs for several thousand years would have destroyed all the protruding parts of the station: radio antennas and reflectors, solar battery panels, etc. After several thousand years, such a station would resemble what Stanislaw Lem described in "Tales of Pirx the Pilot" - NB, this novella exactly matches my hypothesis of a space probe belonging either to the previous Earth SCST or to aliens... - we will return to this topic in future hypotheses. Well, supposedly Stanislaw Lem in the existence of aliens and UFOs did not believe, but this "Tales of Pirx the Pilot" he wrote? He wrote it! To me, all this denial of his is simply hiding in front of the cameras, frolicking with orthodox scholars and an aberration of the great mind that Lem undoubtedly possesses and uses remarkably effectively - for which he is to be commended! "Tales of Pirx the Pilot" does not fit the image of Lem the scoffer or Lem the mocker we know from his novels and short stories - especially "Cyberiad" and the series of stories about Ijon Tichy.

To summarize briefly, this TM could have been a space station that, after many - at least 120 - centuries, drifted gravitationally into the Earth's atmosphere and exploded there. Someone might ask, why there and then? Well," I answer, "because it had to fall somewhere and someday, because this is in accordance with all the laws of celestial mechanics. She fell just as Skylab, Salut or recently Mir fell.[91] The whole difference is that they did not have nuclear devices on board that could have caused the kind of damage that the TCB did.

Nothing was left of the station except the remnants found over Vashka and droplets of metal in the peat bogs of the South Marsh, for what could possibly remain after a thermonuclear explosion estimated at 3...130 Mt TNT? Only an optimist or an idiot could still have any hope that there would be any major debris left after an explosion equal in power to the explosion of tens of millions of tons of 2,4,6-trinitrotoluene! There are no such miracles...

I think it would be a good idea to check whether there were similar accidents behind previous transits of comet P/Halley. It would be necessary to search in the archives, and how about finding something interesting that would be related to this most interesting and longest accompanying comet?...

There is another "cosmic" hypothesis that ties TM to potential aliens. It is:

---

[91] In April 2000, a decision was made to rescue Mir and keep it in its current orbit as an orbital hotel, an idea that was to be financed by a joint Russian-American consortium. That project collapsed and Mir was finally brought down from orbit and burned up in Earth's atmosphere on March 23, 2001, at 06:00 GMT over the Pacific Ocean at Nemo Point.

8.2. Hypothesis #83: The Bracewell probe?

What fell - I'll ask the cursed question here for the umpteenth time - on June 30, 1908, at 00:17.11 GMT, on a point defined by geographic coordinates N 60°55' and E 101°57'? All the theories and hypotheses presented by Wojciechowski and Krassa have some shortcomings, and they don't explain the course changes, and they don't explain - why there was more than one epicenter of the explosion, etc. Hypothesis No. 81 does not explain, for example: why the night sky was observed glowing after the fall of this "satellite of death," while hypothesis No. 82 does not explain such an enormous power of this explosion. Therefore, it occurred to me that what exploded over Podkamennaya Tunguska was a reconnaissance probe from other worlds - the so-called Bracewell probe.

What are Bracewell probes? Let me start by saying that this concept was introduced into ufology and the CETI, SETI and other alien exploration programs in the 1960s, by Australian scientist Prof. Dr. Ronald Bracewell. He came to the conclusion - a reasonable-sounding one, by the way - that the exploration of the Cosmos could be carried out with the help of automated probes or spaceplanes with crews consisting of intelligent machines, which are sent into the Cosmos in the direction of suns suspected of having inhabited planets orbiting around them. Upon arrival in the region of activity of such a CNT, the probe "lurks" and observes this CNT, while sending information to its home planet, - to the CNT that sent it... And so at first the probe automatons carry out reconnaissance under classified surveillance, then - when the CNT in question is already "mature" for it - the surveillance becomes overt. These two stages we know. What will be the next step of the aliens - we can only guess... Who knows if the mysterious circles and pictograms appearing in cereals, corn, oats, millet, rice or grass, and even in snow and on ice are not their work and an attempt at direct contact!?...

And attempts to do so have already taken place, if one counts the strange effects of the experiments of van der Pool and Störmer's first radio probes of the ionosphere in 1926. They received a series of radio echoes in response to their signals, which were tried to interpret in various ways in the 1970s. A young Scottish astronomer from the University of Glasgow - Prof. Dr. Duncan Lunnan - plotted the delays of these mysterious radio echoes and the result was a drawing of the constellation of Volarius with the star ε-Booti or al-Izar or Pulcherrima highlighted on it.

Some time later, the Tallinn-based astronomer Dr. A. V. Spilevskiy turned the chart 90° and obtained a map of the constellation of... Whale, with the star τ-Ceti (Tau Ceti) highlighted on it in turn - distant from us by only 11.85 ly! - i.e. close, for cosmic distances... In turn, the Polish interpreter L. Gorzym from Lublin sees in it a variety of geometric figures and depicted relationships between them...

Personally, I am of the opinion that, during their experiment, van der Pool and Störmer accidentally made contact with the Black Baron, who had already sent a lander to Earth once, and when the latter did not return on June 30, 1908, its automatons waited for signals with which it was only "tinkered" in 1926. They responded using an identical frequency - 9.75 MHz (31.4 m), and

I suspect that these radioechoes were not just simple responses, but multilayered signals of the kind received by the characters in Carl Sagan's novel and the Robert Zemeckis movie based on it, titled "Contact". Then the Black Baron descended from orbit and, under the influence of tidal forces, broke into pieces that slowly fell into the atmosphere and burned, like ordinary meteors.

The Black Baron, or as the Russians prefer it, the Black Prince, was almost perfectly black, i.e. it absorbed 99.99% of the energy falling on its surface, because it was not only about energy intake, but about... camouflage! And yes, because an almost perfectly black body is almost completely invisible in the Cosmos! It becomes visible if and only if it stands against the bright, radiating background of the Sun's or Moon's disk or some nebula. This is what Peter Kolosimo had in mind when he wrote his book "Ombre sulla stelle". This would be an argument for the hypothesis that the Black Baron was a de facto alien reconnaissance probe that attempted to make Contact with us - but...

...but not so long ago, in the monthly magazine "Nieznany Świat" No. 4/2000 there was an article by Adam Mikolajewski titled "Heroes of the Cosmos," in which a list was given of Soviet cosmonauts who either flew into the Cosmos or made ballistic flights, long before the memorable flight of Major Yuri Gagarin on April 12, 1961:

Pilot Pietr Ledowskij - he died during a ballistic flight in 1957;

Pilot Sheborin - he also died under similar circumstances in 1957;

Pilot Mitkow – he died during an attempted orbital flight in 1959;

„Comrade X" - he died under unclear circumstances in May 1960, most likely unable to return to Earth, he committed suicide in orbit. His name was never revealed by the USSR authorities;

Pilot Pyotr Dolgov – he died when a booster exploded on the launch platform in September 1960;

Pilots: Biełokoniew, Koczur and Grachev died in orbit during the first team flight most likely in 1960;

Valentin Bondarenko - he died in a pressure chamber on March 23, 1961;

Vladimir Ilyushin - son of aircraft designer Illyushin - crashes his spacecraft capsule somewhere in the Urals after circling the Earth three times...

... well, and then there was the famous flight of Gagarin, NB, which is also problematic, because as the well-known Hungarian writer István Nemere has shown - Yuri Gagarin was caught in several important inconsistencies that put his flight into question. Besides, in May 1961, two Soviet cosmonauts died in orbit. All this makes it possible to presume that the Black Baron and other pre-1961 NOOs were simply abortive attempts at Soviet space flight!

The hypothesis of a "Bracewell space probe" is supported by psychometric research conducted by Polish ufologist who teaches at colleges in New Zealand, Prof. Dr. Jan Pająk, and Warsaw ufologist Eng. Miloslaw Wilk of the Central Radiation Protection Laboratory, who reconstructed the appearance of the Black Baron and its lander.[92]

And one more thing: such Bracewell probes may operate in the Solar System several, because, I believe, the Cosmos is brimming with life, and no one said that aliens or aliens must be created in our fashion, by identical conditions on their home planets as on Earth. This is what only people without imagination think... Earthlings have been giving the Cosmos a sign of life for more than 100 years on the airwaves. We began experimenting with radio in 1895-1897, while the first transmissions began in 1899. It was like the first cry of a newborn baby!!! The first TV transmissions took place in 1936, and since 1950, the Earth has become the second radio source in the Solar System. If there were any aliens seeing the world with radio waves, they would see three strong radio sources when looking towards the Sun: The Sun, Earth and Jupiter, at which they would immediately realize that Earth's radio emissions are artificial in nature... The Earth is still in an ever swelling bubble of radio radiation that is at least 160 ly in diameter! How many habitable planets could be in a sphere with such a radius of 80 ly? - At least several.

And this is how one should look at the problem.

***

As for my hypotheses, I have tried to embed them in the scientific realities of physics as we know it, although in places I indulge in science-fiction, for I am not obliged by "Occam's razor" - I have not multiplied entities here beyond the need.

---

[92] See K. Bzowski - "Wolf's Web," Rybnik 1999.

8.3. Hypothesis #84: A "visitor" from deep space

It was not a ship, but a flying island, not sure anyway. It was big, from twenty kilometers, like my two fingers - a perfectly regular spindle turned into a disk, no - into a ring!

Of course, you have long thought to yourself that it was a ship of "aliens". Well, since it was ten miles long...

...And I saw in that agonal flash of flare the surface of the giant: its mile-long sidewalls were not smooth, but gnarled, almost like the lunar ground, light spilled over the roughness and debris, crater-like depressions - it must have flown for millions of years like this, entered dark and dead, into dusty nebulae, exited them after centuries, and meteorite dust in tens of thousands of collisions gobbled it up and nibbled it with vacuum erosion...

We had a visitor from the Cosmos, a visitation, occurring - I don't know? - once in millions, no - hundreds of millions of years... passed through our fingers to dissolve like a ghost, into infinite space...

Stanisław Lem - „Tales of Pirx the Pilot"

...Let's start with some facts that constitute scientific heresy - I'm talking about the fall of meteorites that do not belong to our Solar System - non-solar system meteorites.

What is the point? Orthodox science claims that there are no non-solar system meteorites. They simply do not exist, period.[93] I

---

[93] Not true - this is contradicted by the recent discoveries of several off-system objects like 'Oumuamua, Borisov's comet or the IM1 and IM2

have no idea why scientists claim that there is no right to have them - after all, there is a flow of matter between stars, and if so, some part of this matter must flow in the form of just meteorites, comets and other "junk". Such "junk" was the recently observed comet Hayakutake, which visited us in 1995/96.

Astronomers found that it had a chemical composition similar to systemic comets, but... the ratio of HCN to R-CN was completely different from that in "regular" comets, and this indicated its alien origin. R-CN radicals were more than 1,000 times more than regular.

So, TM could have been such a "visitor" from deep Space, whose chemical composition did not at all correspond to the chemical composition of "our" meteors, and at the moment of entering the Earth's atmosphere with a hyperbolic velocity Vg >> VIII and at a small angle, a thermonuclear reaction could have occurred in it, that is, the fusion of hydrogen atoms into a single helium atom with the release of massive amounts of energy. The powerful thrust of the Earth's atmosphere created the right conditions for the reaction, i.e. a high temperature of about 1 million K and a pressure of one million Pa, which led to a hydrogen-helium conversion reaction, according to equations:

1. $2H \rightarrow He + \beta+ + \nu + 1,44\,MeV$
2. $22H \rightarrow H + 3H + 3,25\,MeV$
3. $22H \rightarrow 3He + n + 4\,MeV$
4. $2H + 3H \rightarrow He + n + 17,6\,Mev$

meteorites...

5. $4H \rightarrow He + 2\beta- + 26\,MeV$

And in the aftermath to the explosion of the meteorite like a several-megaton hydrogen bomb with known consequences. This hypothesis is good insofar as it agrees with the observations made by Polish astronomers regarding the existence of swarms of non-solar system meteorites. In light of this, TM was simply a lump of "dirty" ice that flew through the Cosmos at a speed of >100 km/s, and from the Sun!

Thus, there was a density of Solar System planets along TM's path and there was also our central star, and yet TM just hit the Earth!!! To me, this is an indication that there is no natural astronomical body, and that TM just flew towards Earth, on which it ended its flight! Now I think you understand, Reader, the motto for this subsection. Stanislaw Lem, with all his ridiculous disbelief in the existence of UFOs, hints at the possibility of meeting if not aliens, then the remaining artifacts of them, and personally I would not be surprised if the situation described by him in this story becomes a reality in 25, 50 or 100 years!

Related to the above is my next hypothesis:

8.4. Hypothesis #85: Return from the stars

They watched in silence. Shifting on the screen, the image peeking out from under the clouds was very different from the shapes retained in memory. Some of the continents had disappeared, their place taken by seas dotted with archipelagos of islands. They waited anxiously for the land and city from which their ship had once launched into Space to appear. The image moved slowly, the planet revealing more and more surface details. The first clenched his fingers on the armchair's railing and leaned toward the screen's surface. The clocks ticked away the time.

The First's face turned pale; he covered his eyes. Where there should have been a large continent, there was only the sea, the ocean and nothing else...

Witold Zegalski - „Return of the Giants"

It assumes that the SCST of Atlantis, which existed on Earth in the distant past, was so technically advanced that it could afford to send manned or automated interstellar probes toward the nearest suns hoping to have their own planetary systems. These vehicles took off and at low travel speeds - at any rate, non-relativistic and therefore <0.5c flew into Space, to return to Earth after a few thousand years.

12,000 years ago, the Atlantean civilization crashed and Mankind regressed to the Stone Age. Meanwhile, crews sent to

Space at the earliest began to return. The only thing is that they had nowhere to return to, because all the space installations of Earth and other colonized planets were destroyed or out of order. Those who managed to land, the primitive inhabitants of Earth gave a ceremonial welcome, because in their mind they were dealing with gods... Thus, there were no aliens in the history of our civilization - there were only people who could merge with other people and thus revive Humanity. And that's it! Subsequent landing crews were taken over by an organization that ensured that the cosmonauts adapted to the changed conditions - this is Freemasonry... And this is all the Knowledge, which, for the little ones, is transmitted by means of symbols and esoteric language incomprehensible to the layman. And this is the purpose and meaning of the existence of this organization. In this context, the efforts of alchemists to transform one element into another, the search for alkathest, ether or panacea and the production of homunculus, which were nothing but biological robots - neuromats - become understandable... Understandable is the secrecy shrouded in all the activities of the Brothers of the Lodge and the Ansamblei - because the Rosicrucians are also involved - which is necessary because the ancient cosmonauts are the core of the Brotherhood and only they have the knowledge, but they do not have the machinery park, which they have yet to create - and they created it virtually from nothing...

In Africa, there is a people who explicitly claim about themselves that they come from the stars - specifically, from one star - the Alpha of the Little Dog - Sirius. They are the Dogon people. Their knowledge is puzzling, so some titled buffoon came up with the hypothesis that they were told about the ballet of

Sirius by some white traveler or merchant who happened to be there, and so these dark and uncultured Negroes took it for granted and immediately in their stupidity identified with the story until they created a cult... - enough with the bullshit! Wouldn't it be better, and applying Occam's razor, to assume that the Dogon people are simply the descendants of Atlantean ancient astronauts, who have been thrashing around in Space for several thousand years and returned to Earth, ravaged after a thermonuclear war? Having no way to let them know about themselves and their journey, they had to create a religious myth that included elements of their knowledge and at the same time their story of their space Odyssey... How simple it is - isn't it? Well, but this we understand now - at the beginning of the 21st century, when one little thing remains a mystery - how these Protodogons were able to fly to Sirius and return to Earth???!!! Because they did it, which is beyond discussion - the only question left is: how?

In this view, TM is just such a spaceship of the Atlanteans, which in 1908 returned to Earth, or rather, crashed, unable to land on the sands of the Gobi desert. The first expedition that went into the taiga did a cleanup there after the crash, because its members knew what to look for and what to hide from outsiders' eyes...

This clue was suggested to me by Stanislaw Lem in his novel "Return from the Stars" and Witold Zegalski in the short story "Return of the Giants" quoted here,[94] in which he writes about such a return from the stars in the context of TM!!! Intuition? - or

---

[94] In the anthology "Message from the Fifth Planet", Warsaw 1964.

perhaps crumbs of Secret Knowledge of the Freemason Brothers???...

Thus, there are no aliens! It's a bit of a shame, because this is a beautiful dream and it's hard to give it up... However, I still hope that I am wrong and some aliens will eventually come to us. Recently the media reported that the Americans will make public what they know about UFOs in 2010. Hmmm... - I suspect that this truth may just look like what I've described here - assuming the truth is published at all, and we're not lulled into another putty of the kind of curmudgeonly document titled "NASA's Statement on the Existence of UFOs" from 1999, which stated that UFOs are the latest generation of military machines...[95]

And to conclude with two more made-up hypotheses. Doing a translation of the already mentioned here study by Peter Krassa entitled "Tunguska, das rätselfafte Jahrhunderteignis" I was amazed to read there and such a passus:

Margareta Schneider from Bonn has, despite her will, created another hypothesis about the etiology of TP herself. Working in the embassy of the former West Germany in China, she became very familiar with spoken and written Chinese. In one of her letters to me, she wrote:

«I would not hesitate to say that if it was a spaceplane, it most likely could have originated in China. There is a possibility that Chinese scholars constructed such a vehicle to escape the uprising in their country at the time...[96]

---

[95] The Americans actually gave some facts to the public and that UFOs/UAPs actually exist in 2023.

[96] This refers to **Sun Yat-sena's** uprising, which culminated in the

I have at my disposal a tripartite Chinese-German-English dictionary by Richard Wilhelm published in 1912, which contains all the basic words and concepts of nuclear physics in Chinese ideograms. The uranium deposits are located in Mongolia (Ulanbaatar)»[97]

Margaret Schneider did not hide the fact that her theory has its weak points, but compared to recent hypotheses it can be considered to be correct. Let's recall the marsh gas explosion hypotheses...

N Well, I laughed heartily, albeit unkindly. Until one day. In June 2001, I bought Hartwig Hausdorf's book titled "The 20th century, a century of mysteries and phenomena" (Warsaw 2001), which included brief descriptions of 100 of the most mysterious events of the last century. There was also a chapter titled "Alchemist awakens the forces of the atom," in which it stated - and I quote accurately - that:

About 40 years ago, nuclear weapons specialists from the People's Liberation Army were tasked with testing nuclear weapons in a desert area near the Mongolian border. To their surprise, they discovered there calcified tree trunks and soil melted to glass - unmistakable signs of a nuclear explosion. However, in those years - let alone before - no one had conducted such tests there. It wasn't until October 16, 1964 that the People's

---

proclamation of the republic in 1911.

[97] At that time Urga, today Ulan Bator. The uranium ore deposits are located on the Russian side of the border, in Zakamensk. In Mongolia, there are small deposits of uranium ores accompanying the lead ore deposits in the East Gobi Aymak.

Republic of China joined as the fifth member of the elite club of nuclear powers.

The military thus faced quite a mystery. They conducted detailed research and undertook an investigation among local residents. This is what they discovered: back at the beginning of the 20th century, a certain man had managed to unleash the forces hidden in the nucleus of the atom!

A whole string of clues and hypotheses led the investigators to the track of a scientist named Pou Chao-fi - an alchemist - who built himself a laboratory near a standing pagoda. He read information in ancient texts that allowed him to trigger a chain reaction. The construction of an atomic bomb is quite simple - all you need is a few pure ingredients, which have to be added together in the right order.

Old peasants in the 1950s recalled a strange event that took place on July 8, 1910. On that very day, an extremely violent detonation occurred in the pagoda area. The explosion was so powerful that it was heard within a radius of 600 kilometers.

In the archives of the library in Beijing, it was possible to find drawings made by the hand of a forgotten genius. Based on them, scientists came to the unequivocal conclusion that he had already studied powerful forces several decades earlier, from which he finally died. In his notes, Pou Chao-fi described "a terrifying fire from the sky, which is produced by the compression of metal atoms."

The courageous scientist dealt with more than just the theoretical side of the issue. Eventually, disaster came. Pou Chao-fi lost his life in a powerful explosion that destroyed not only his laboratory and pagoda, but also vegetation within a radius of many kilometers. The great researcher, who decades before the Hiroshima tragedy unleashed the power of the atom, should be considered the first victim of nuclear weapons testing.

Sure, but not everything. For I suspect that Pou Chao-fi got his hands on Atlantean or alien technology - some kind of artifact like the "Košice radio-artifact" - with which he built a primitive nuclear bomb, which he detonated. That "fire from the sky"! Could it have come from a space object sprayed in the atmosphere that fell to Earth two years earlier? This would mean that the TCB was some kind of spacecraft after all!!!...

9. R. Leśniakiewicz, K. Piechota, B. Rzepecki - TM ALLA POLACCA

Leaving aside the literary aspect of TM's fall, which in Poland was also exploited in SF and adventurous-travel literature - to mention just one of the novels by A. Szklarski - "Tomek's secret expedition" - here we would like to mention some mysterious events that took place in the years after World War II, which to this day have not found any satisfactory explanation. We are referring, of course, to the fall (???) of the Great Polish Bolide (hereafter GPB) on August 20, 1979, the fall and explosion of the mysterious something that, for lack of a better term, we will call the Jerzmanowice Unusual Thing on January 14, 1993, which incidents we will take up first. Both of these events bear all the hallmarks of TP - as we will discuss below. And so far no one has provided a rational explanation for these phenomena, so that we are doomed only to conjecture...

9.1. The Great Polish Bolide

In August 1979, Robert was still a cadet of the fourth year of the General Tadeusz Kościuszko Higher School of Mechanized Forces in Wrocław and was undergoing specialized training at the

Border Protection Forces Training Center in Kętrzyn.[98] Therefore, he learned about the GPB flight from his colleagues: Sgt. Cadet Kazimierz G. from Poznań, Sgt. Cadet Mark B. from Wrocław, and Sgt. Cadet Zbigniew D. from Sandomierz, who were returning to Kętrzyn from a trip to Reszel. They later told him that they saw some luminous bodies constituting a swarm of sparks - "like from a steam locomotive" - moving rapidly against the background of the evening aurora from north to south-southwest. Then he recalled that he too had seen something similar from Kętrzyn.

Of course, he didn't worry too much about it, because he wasn't up to it; in a week's time, promotion to first officer rank, moving to a new place of duty in the Pomeranian WOP Brigade in Szczecin - that was the most important thing. And it wasn't until 1985 that he remembered it, when he contacted Bronislaw Rzepecki and Krzysztof Piechota - who had researched the case - and read another volume of Lucjan Znicz-Sawicki's "Visitors from Space - NOL," which accurately described the GPB overflight based on eyewitness accounts. According to what the doyen of Polish ufology wrote, GPB came from the N-NW direction and flew over Poland heading S-SE (trajectory no. 1), flew over the border of Poland and the former ČSRS, flew further over the territory of Slovakia further towards Ukraine.

---

[98] Until 1989, WSOWZmech. Educated officer cadres for the WOP. After 2 years in Wrocław, the cadets were detached to CS WOP Kętrzyn. Today there is the headquarters of the Mazurian-Podlasie Branch of the Border Guard.

According to the second version given by the Poznań astronomer Dr. H. Kuzminski, GPB came from the NW direction and flew in the SE direction (trajectory No. 2), flying over the territory of Ukraine, over which it ended its days by falling into dust...

However, the most interesting thing was ahead, because Krzysztof and Bronisław took up the matter once again, reexamined all available witness accounts and, based on them, plotted their own version of the GPB trajectory (trajectory No. 3), diametrically opposed to what was known so far...[99] It looked as if the GPB had made as many as two maneuvers in the air while flying over Poland:

Maneuver No. 1 - a turn of almost 90o to the west in flight over the vicinity of Elbląg in the direction of Toruń, and...

...Maneuver No. 2 - a 90o turn to the east in flight over Toruń towards Przemyśl...

Such a thing cannot be done by any bolide - and therefore GPB could not be any bolide!

So what was it?

Krzysztof Piechota thinks it was a space container containing nutrients that greatly influenced the appearance of the so-called "crop failure" of agricultural crops in Poland in the 1980s, despite the collapsing planned economy. He believes that this was a kind of experiment conducted on our nation, which then brought out Solidarity in 1980 and began to subvert communism. The analogy

---

[99] They published the results in "NOL" No. 1/1990 and "UFO" No. 2(10)/1992.

was clear - in 1908 the TM flew over and in 1917 the Tsar in Russia fell. In 1979, GPB flew over Poland and other Central European countries and communism collapsed in Europe in 1989. Therefore, could it be a socio-technical experiment of aliens or Gaia - our Mother-Earth? - Which, paradoxically, is much more likely than alien intervention from deep space!...

Robert Leśniakiewicz, for his part, put forward a counter-hypothesis proclaiming that the GPB was nothing more than an ICBM missile launched from the deck of an American or Soviet missile submarine, e.g., due to an error in the computers directing the firing of missiles from its deck, or a failure of the launcher. This ICBM was fired in the Norwegian Sea and flew over Norway further over Sweden, the Baltic Sea, Poland, Ukraine and fell into the Black Sea near Varna or Constanta, or went out to LEO and stayed there..[100] Everything pointed to it: the twisted trajectory of the GPB's flight, the upward trajectory rather than the downward trajectory, the report of a sighting of a strange "old Russian intercontinental missile" over the Swedish naval base in Karlskrona, which was observed by a missile warfare officer from the JW KA-1 fortress rocket artillery crew, Col. Lars-Ove Forsberg[101], as well as information about soil contamination and radiation poisoning of Hungarian construction workers working on the installation of the Hungarian Orenburg Pipeline, in September 1979.[102] Given the account of Colonel Forsberg's sighting, one

---

[100] This hypothesis was published in "UFO" No. 3,1990 and in the book "UFO over the border" (Kraków 2000).

[101] Name changed at the request of the witness. This information comes from Swedish ufologist **Clasa Svahna**.

must assume that the GPB performed two evasive maneuvers over the Baltic - if it had not done so, it would have flown over the territory of our country somewhere in the vicinity of Kołobrzeg. Thus, it follows that this GPB behaved in the air like a guided missile, or like a Cruise missile, which wanted to avoid being tracked by both Swedish, Danish and NATO and Polish and Soviet radiolocation stations! - Which is evident from the graph of its trajectory...

However, the ICBM hypothesis collapses, because so far (July 2023) neither side has admitted to firing this missile, yet US or Soviet/Russian propaganda would have raised a furore in such a case. How much of an outcry there would have been in "Free Europe" or "Voice of America" - meanwhile, there was nothing of the sort... - ergo - it was not a Soviet "nuke"!

It could have been a "nuke" but not a Soviet or American one, but... cosmic! After all, GPB fits the theory of atomic wars of god-astronauts from 12,000 years ago, which we have already referred to in previous chapters. Or maybe it was just a meteorite after all, but why then did it change the trajectory of its flight as many as four times???... How was this even possible?

The most interesting thing is that our Hungarian friend - the president of the Hungarian UFO Research Federation in Debrecen Dr. Eng. Gábor Tarcali gave us a signal about the contamination in Ukraine, which was suffered by Hungarians working there. At first, Soviet physicians had pushed it on them that they had been infected with some endemic infection in Ukraine, but when it turned out to be radiation sickness, they

---

[102] Information given by the Hungarian press in 1990.

were sent back to Hungary with a punch. These workers succumbed to contamination with isotopes of plutonium - Pu and americium - Am. And here the question should be asked: was it plutonium and americium from the shattered warheads of an ancient intercontinental missile? Or was it a nuclear power plant accident hidden from the world? Such a possibility is real, for the USSR authorities hid environmental disasters from the world just as an Indian hides his fear and a white man hides his sins...

Another signal came from Slovakia, where in Košice, in the city's catacombs, a mysterious box of dark metal covered with mysterious inscriptions in Latin letters, but in an unknown language, and whose contents were highly radioactive, was uncovered. Five workers succumbed to radiation poisoning and were hospitalized, while the box was taken away by the army in an unknown direction! - and all hearing of it was lost... The case was investigated by well-known Slovak ufologist Dr. Miloš Jesenský, who concluded that it could have been a box containing the highly radioactive isotope plutonium - 238Pu+IV, which is used in nuclear warheads. The box is gone, and the curious thing is that the military or the police have not admitted to knowing anything about it!!! Could it be that the Lodge Brothers are at work again? In November 2000, during the IX Central European Ufological Congress, we talked about this issue with a journalist of the newspaper "Košice večer", editor Miroslav Sambor, who said that the whole affair was just a hoax plotted to increase the newspaper's print circulation. OK, maybe that's true - but in view of the above, why was the place where the box was found in the Košice catacombs thoroughly isolated from the rest of the world by bricking up all the entrances leading to it with a wall two bricks thick? To this Editor Sambor was no longer able to give a meaningful answer. We visited the underground in September 1996 with Marian Książek and saw the still fresh cement cementing the bricks and stones together.[103] We regretted that we didn't have a G-M counter, because we could have checked the radiation level of the area around the mysterious room...

Anyway, the Košice radio-artifact really exists, and Someone was very anxious that it should not fall into the hands of too inquisitive researchers... From all this, it is indisputable that ancient peoples collected plutonium from the earth-shattering unexploded nuclear warheads of the Atlanteans and used them for their purposes! Perhaps the Celts, who inhabited these lands, did so, as evidenced by the story of the Košice radioactive box...

Let's return to the ICBM version of the GPB. In the picture we see a diagram of the course of events on the critical evening of August 20, 1979. The first visual contact was made with the GPB at 20:35 CEST or 18:35 GMT - point "a" on the diagram. The GPB then disintegrated into a warhead and anti-radiation cloaking measures - point "b" - which formed a radioactive layer over the Coast - "c" - At the same time, it began to perform an evasive maneuver. This maneuver ended near Toruń - point "d" - the warhead returned to its old course after performing a second evasive maneuver. About 70 seconds after entering over Polish territory, the warhead leaves its borders - point "e" - over the Bieszczady Mountains flying over Ukraine, breaking up in the air

---

[103] The whole affair was described by Dr. Miloš Jesenský in the pages of "Nieznany Świat" No. 4/1997.

"f" into debris "g", which falls either on Ukrainian territory or into the Black Sea basin.

This figure explains approximately how the GPB flew over Poland. It is evident that it attempted to avoid entering the field of view of NATO and Swedish naval radiolocation stations. It also avoided Polish and Soviet anti-aircraft, naval and WOP radars. The latter could target air targets, but flying up to a ceiling of 2,400 meters.

The GPB flew further south-southeast breaking up and sowing around with radioisotopes 239Pu, 240Pu, 238Am, 239Am and others, which were found in the soil of Ukraine even before the Chernobyl disaster! Isn't it a proof that GPB was not something belonging to our civilization!?...

And again we return to the theme of the existence of one or even several Super-Civilizations of Science and Technology before us... Recently, in the pages of various exo- and esoteric magazines, this has been proven by an underestimated by his titled colleagues Polish scientist, Professor of the University of Szczecin Prof. Dr. Benon Zbigniew Szałek, who, using his brilliant analytical methods, proved directly that there once existed on Earth a mother civilization that used one language and one - almost unified - script! Traces of it have been found in the Mediterranean, the Indus Valley and Easter Island! And the whole problem is that Prof. Szałka's smart-mouthed colleagues refuse to accept this simple fact and come up with all sorts of twisted theories just to avoid admitting that an outsider with an academic title is right...

We believe that GPB is just one link in a long chain of evidence of the existence of our ancestors, whose technical capabilities created them as gods of our planet!...

9.2. Jerzmanowice

This was the strangest and most TM fall-like event we have encountered in our ufological career. The Jerzmanowice Incident - or rather, the fall of the Jerzmanowice Unusual Thing (because it cannot be called otherwise) phenomenally reminds us of the fall of TCB - only that the scale of the phenomenon was incomparably smaller: over Podkamiennaya Tunguska tore 13...130 Mt of 2,4,6-trinitrotoluene, while in Jerzmanowice the load amounted to only 80-100 kg of TNT - that is, 1.3 million times less! But this in no way reduces the importance and spectacularity of the phenomenon!...

On the subject of the Jerzmanowitzkie Unusual Thing - hereinafter JUT - probably everything has already been written. Military specialists and university professors have studied it. They have come up with nothing. No meteorite remains were found - because it was assumed a priori, it is not clear why, that it was a meteorite - nor a missile, as the military assumed. The situation reminds us exactly of a cross between a Czech and a Soviet movie: "there was something and there is not - and nobody knows anything...".

And it was like this:

On the evening of January 14, 1993, at about 19:00 CET (18:00 GMT), the residents of Jerzmanowice near Kraków (Kraków county, Małopolskie voivodeship) were roused by a strange phenomenon - well, something hit into the limestone outcrop called Babia Góra and smashed its top into small pebbles, which littered the ground in a radius of 700 meters from it along an uneven ellipse of spread. The blast wave blew out windows within a kilometer radius of the epicenter, while the rumble of the explosion was heard even in Kraków and Sosnowiec. The explosion was accompanied by a flash, which was observed in Zawoja, 67 kilometers away.

The explosion caused panic among people and livestock. A moment afterwards, people smelled a suffocating odor, as if of pesticides - something like DDT or another pesticide based on it. The explosion caused animals to react aggressively or apathetically, while humans became apathetic and slowed their reflexes. It lasted for almost a week.

A strange thing - the explosion caused the burning of all light bulbs and electrical appliances - even those that were not turned on - within a radius of 1 km from the epicenter of the explosion. This resembled quite closely the phenomena accompanying the explosion of the Tomsk (Chulimsky) Meteorite on February 26, 1984. However, here we are dealing with a phenomenon much smaller in scale...

As you can see, the fall and explosion of JUT comes out pretty poorly compared to the other phenomena, but... So far, no one has given a reason for this phenomenon, and scholars have fail in JUT, just as they have on TP. Ufologists too...

JUT began to be investigated relatively late, because only in the spring of 1999, when a team from the Malopolska Research Center for UFOs and Anomalous Phenomena appeared in Jerzmanowice, consisting of: Anna and Robert Leśniakiewicz, Marzena, Ewelina and Wioletta Wójtowicz, and Bartosz Soczówka with his father. First, however, there was an analysis of all the information collected, from which it appeared that JUT, if it was a meteorite at all, was a strange one indeed! It was impossible to determine the direction from which this meteorite came over the impact site in Jerzmanowice. Some witnesses said from the west, others said from the east or northeast.

Astronomers said that the JUT could have been associated with asteroid 6344 P-L, which happened to be passing through its perigee on January 14, 1993, and it could have come from the NE direction.

In turn, the military searched the area around Babia Góra and Sikorka rocks, because according to the military, the object came from the direction of Kraków, 19 km away... In a word, even this has not been established unquestionably, because although the ellipse of the scattering of debris of the peak of Babia Góra pointed in favor of the latter version, other accounts indicate that it was quite different...

The mysterious thing is that moments before the explosion, witnesses stated a plane flew over the area, which gave rise to claims that it was the military that lost something there that should not be seen by civilian eyes - in a word, the Polish "X-Files"!? What could it have been? A hundred-kilogram air bomb or missile warhead, or perhaps a mysterious E-weapon -

incapacitating all electrical and electronic systems, which the USAF and NATO air force used during the Kosovo war in 1999?[104]

A lightning strike? Why not? A cold atmospheric front from over Scandinavia was moving and an electrical storm developed. The discharge hit the top of Babia Góra and caused an electrical explosion of water lingering in its crevices... Beautiful! - only that through and through untrue, because according to witnesses, the peak of Babia Mountain was never struck by lightning, and even if it was, the electricity would have flowed down the rock without penetrating it. Thus, there was no electric rainstorm - and there could not have been. Unexpected confirmation of the "lightning" hypothesis was provided by the seismograph recordings from the seismological station of the Polish Academy of Sciences in Ojców, where at 18h58m54s and 19h00m17s CET on the critical day, two tremors were recorded that were similar to those produced by lightning striking rock. Doesn't this fit like a glove with the phenomena accompanying the fall and explosion of TM???

There is another hypothesis - quite crazy, but... The idea is that someone may have tested the workings of a small nuclear warhead - something à la the American W-88, NB, the plans of which were stolen by the Chinese from the Americans a few years ago. Such a small nuke , which supposedly can be put in a briefcase, and of which more than a dozen - there is talk of 100 - were lost from the Russians' nuclear arsenals.[105] It would be an

---

[104] Currently, everything indicates that it was an E-bomb accidentally dropped on Jerzmanowice.

[105] **R. Bernatowicz & W. Łuczak** - „Nautilius Radia Zet", broadcast in april 2001.

ideal weapon in the hands of terrorists and mafia - I don't even mention special forces... So maybe someone planted such a charge - a micro nuclear charge - in Jerzmanowice? But actually why just there?! I know a few other and more interesting places in this country - just, for example, in Warsaw at Wiejska Street! I'm afraid, however, that such a "mother" (that's licencia poetica from Stanislaw Lem - sic!) would have a power of at least several kt TNT, while in Jerzmanowice only 0.00001 kt TNT exploded - a bit too much for our taste. Not to mention that the neutron flash created at the time of the thermonuclear explosion and further amplified by the so-called "red mercury" RM 20/20[106] would finish off everything living within at least a kilometer radius... It would be reasonable to assume, that all the energy of the explosion was converted not into a stream of neutrons, but into a powerful magnetic pulse that electrocuted all electrical and electronic equipment within a 1,000-meter radius of the epicenter. This would be an ideal weapon to blind the enemy's radar and other sensors. Has anyone tried this weapon - later used in the Persian Gulf against Iraq, Bosnia and Herzegovina and in Kosovo by NATO and USAF air forces - on the residents of Jerzmanowice? I don't think so - although under the conditions of the prevailing mess and lawlessness in the Third Brightest Polish Republic, even such things are possible... Perhaps this weapon slipped out of someone's hands, and that is what is most likely to happen![107]

---

[106] The so-called "red mercury" is a compound with the chemical formula $Hg_2Sb_2O_6$-7, which most likely acts as a neutron duplicator. Subsequent searches revealed that the whole case is a hoax and RM 20/20 does not actually exist.

But is it true?

We don't think it's untrue, because there is a possibility that the close passage near Earth of an asteroid designated 6344 P-L could have knocked down an orbiting armed satellite of the US, Russia, China or... Atlantis! The point is that there have been more such events in world history.

This is only a modest slice of what is happening above and around us... - but we don't think Mankind had E-weapons back in the 17th century! So this must be another trace and at the same time proof of the reality of the atomic wars of the ancient gods-astronauts!...

And now seemingly on another subject. On November 7, 1996, a strange event occurred in Olsztyn near Częstochowa. At about 04:00 in the morning its residents were awakened by a terrible bang. Several witnesses saw a brightly lit UAP appear next to the castle tower. This was followed by a second one that landed near the castle ruins. This mysterious nighttime mystery lasted about half an hour, after which both UAPs disappeared.

The site was first inspected two weeks after that CE2 by Bronislaw Rzepecki and Marian Książek, who found the presence of strange circles - or rather rings of fresh - as if spring - grass with spring flowers and fungi of the species of the livid entoloma - Entoloma sinutatum, which occurs only in spring - in May and early June! It looked as if time had gone backwards or sped up to spring in these unusual rings. These rings - or rather, formations resembling the shape of an elongated letter C - were about 5

---

[107] And unfortunately that's exactly what happened!

meters long and 70 centimeters wide. The grass on these sites was noticeably bushier, and when we were last there on August 7, 1999, they were still clearly visible.

And interestingly enough, similar grass rings were also found at UAP landing sites in Hungary and Romania - as Gábor Tarcali of HUFORF informed us. We also saw something similar here in Poland at the UAP landing site on Mt. Golgota, near the village of Spytkowice (Nowy Targ district, Małopolskie voivodeship), where the UAP left behind three rings of fresh grass and an isosceles triangle. Here, too, we found a huge outpouring of livid entoloma, which in May formed so-called "black circles" of their fruiting bodies there. I refer those interested to the study "PROJECT TATRA - Final Report", where the whole thing is described.

In May 1999, during a site visit, the CBZA team discovered in a meadow at the foot of Babia Góra the same green grass ring that Rzepecki and Książek discovered in 1996 in Olsztyn near Częstochowa. In April 2000, two of our colleagues from CBZA Podkarpacie: Arkadiusz Miazga and Marcin Mierzwa from Ropczyce discovered a large grassy ring located about 7 km east of Brzesko, just off Road 4 (E-40). The visible half-circle of grass is about 15.3 meters in diameter, and it is most likely that an UAP or UFO landing took place there!

Four grass-ring sites have been discovered in the Ropczyce area, as recently reported to us by another CBZA Podkarpacie member, Grzegorz Dawid.

In all of these cases mentioned here, it was dark green, fresh grass outgrowing last year's dried out blades! Identical to the CE2 site in Spytkowice! So, was there an UAP crash in Jerzmanowice, rather than an explosion of the remnants of the Great Gods-Astronauts Conflict? No such grass rings were found at the site of the TM drop, but did anyone look for them there? - as far as we know, no one!...

Robert searched for similar circles in the Tatra Mountains, in the area of Giewont, Czerwone Wierchy and Kominiarski Wierch (Kominy Tylkowe) - to no avail. He did not find a single one there. So it seems that UAPs did not land there - which, admittedly, was not confirmed by the results of PROJECT TATRY - or something else landed there, but what? We don't know... So far no one has any reasonable idea.

There is another interesting aspect of this case: the presence of UOO and... post-volcanic sites in the NW areas of the Lesser Poland province.

UOOs - these are Unknown Orbital Objects that have been observed for a long time. It's not just Dr. Bagby's Black Baron. It's a whole bunch of observations made during three years by CBZA and other organizations and individual researchers from Warsaw, Wrocław, Kłodzko and the Coast. UOO and JUT are linked by their origin in the Cosmos. In turn, this is related to the fact that there are post-volcanic areas in the vicinity of Alwernia, Krzeszowice and Regulice - and these are from 200 million years ago - and under Krzeszowice there was a huge volcanic caldera with a diameter of 25 km, and there are thermals there... Yes, as in the case of TM fall! The volcanic traps of Podkamennaya Tunguska are also 200 million years old - so if this is just a coincidence, it is extremely strange!...

There is also the other side of this coin - well, before the outbreak of World War III and in the first days of its duration[108], The area around Alwernia was penetrated by UAPs, while the night sky over Lesser Poland was crossed every now and then by UOOs. In the quarries of Alwernia and Regulice, melaphyrs and tuffs (fossilized tephra) are broken, in which amethysts can sometimes be found. Their purple coloration - as in the case of halite (rock salt) - indicates that they have been subjected to α, β and γ radiation, which most likely comes from hydrothermal deposits of uranium-thorium ores, which, in turn, aliens from UFOs are keeping an eye on? It's possible, because aliens are keeping a close eye on the mining, processing and utilization of Earth's energy resources. Most likely, in order to assess our economic and, consequently, military capabilities, and the potential possibility of destroying our planet or Theirs... This matter was studied by Tomasz Niesporek and Jerzy Strzeja of the Katowice-based "Sieci" and they are of a similar opinion. Well, but this is already a topic for a separate study.

To sum up, our reality, which is so well known, hides from us the second and third bottom - and that is the Presence of aliens on our planet. Reading Wojciechowski's study, you get the impression that something was left unsaid until the end and the entire study was not completed. All attempts to explain the TP boiled down or sooner or later to one thing: TM was certainly of cosmic origin, and the only thing missing was the one and only

---

[108] This is about the Kosovo war of 1999-2000, which involved 26 countries from three continents, so this war can be called a world war, because it went beyond Europe...

statement that TM was of artificial origin... Scientists were afraid, are afraid, and will be afraid for a long time to come of such definite-sounding statements, because they would have to take as an absolute certainty either the fact of the existence of an alien CNT operating in the Solar System, or the fact of the existence of a remnant of the SCST that preceded us, which perhaps now already operates in the open Cosmos! - and no self-respecting, orthodox scientist would allow himself such a far-fetched conclusion... And yet there are artifacts - tangible evidence that either (or even both) of these possibilities is true! A classic, even clinical example of such artifacts are the ones I present below. The first photo shows an object 8 cm in diameter, and the relief covering it most likely represents... a diagram of the solar system, or some other planetary system... The second photo came to us from Japan, and it shows a spherical artifact from a temple museum in Nara. Could this "cult object" be a model of... of an alien planet???...

As has been said here many times, traces of the stay and activity on Earth of the native SCST can be seen at every turn, and it is only to the fact that they are so common that we do not notice them... - and that's where all the misery lies. TM is one link in a long chain of puzzles that includes megalithic buildings, UFOs, Earth's chakras, the capabilities of the human body and mind, religions of East and West, etc. - all these have their roots in the distant past of our species *Homo sapiens sapiens*...

We are convinced that when we take the next step into Space and start exploring the Moon and its vicinity, we will certainly find artifacts from our Earthly SCST, and who knows if not from aliens too... We hope that we will encounter living beings, and not just automatons left over from the Great God-Astronaut Conflict of a hundred and twenty centuries ago - and which may have evolved to become half-living half-mechanical beings like the Destroyers and Zlywrogs from Sergey Sniegov's novel "Far Journeys" or semi-automatic beings straight out of Steven Spielberg's and George Lucas' films.

Everything points to the fact that this is what happened...

And the evidence? - someone will ask. The evidence is all around us, only we do not always want to see it. Take, for example, the mysterious stone balls found here and there in the rocks of the Beskydy Mountains or the Slovakian Javorniki. To this day, no one has given a reasonable explanation as to their origin. Scientists are coming up with ever more reckless hypotheses that, instead of brightening the picture, only obscure it. They babble something incoherent about concretions at the bottom of the Tethys Ocean or spherical weathering... Robert Leśniakiewicz once threw out a hypothesis that these were meteorites that reached the Earth and penetrated deep into the clay and salt sediments at the bottom of the drying Tethys Ocean... But no, this hypothesis collapsed in the heat of factual analysis. They cannot be meteorites if only because they are the most normal Earth sandstones...

Therefore, we suspect that the intelligent automatons left after the Conflict gradually became independent from mongrels with animals and completely primitive humans, by creating their own energy and renovation base. What does a robot need to survive – that is. actively interfere with the surrounding environment? Three things, namely:

Energy sources;

Spare parts;

Repair and overhaul workshops.

After the Great Conflict of the Gods, only intelligent machines remained, subject to no one - with few exceptions. Who ruled in Ancient times? Kings? - No. Chiefs - neither. Oligarchy? - they only seemed to rule over people thanks to the fortunes they possessed. Only those who possessed ancient knowledge - mages and priests - ruled. It was magic and religion - exactly in that order - that allowed them to hold power over the mob. Dark, unenlightened, but constituting a blind force, the motley crowd could be exploited and was used for their purposes. It was the mages and priests who held power over demons and other supernatural forces. Forget about demons! - It was over these robots that no one could - except them - direct anymore. These very robots were demons that could be controlled with the help of spells - or rather, commands given to them in a language they understood - such as Atlantean! Looking at the disk from Phaistos (Faistos), Robert Leśniakiewicz has the impression that he is looking at... a modern CD-rom with a program for a computer or other rational machine loaded into it! What ever you call it, it's all about - as Prof. Szałek discovered - the language that was spoken during the rise and fall of the Supercivilization of the Atlantean Empire! So, all those key-words like "abracadabra," "hokey-pokey", etc. are nothing but specific messages intended for Atlantean machines, computers and neuromats. And this is where the power of the great mages of Ancient times - who were simply the descendants of Atlantean computer scientists and cyberneticians - came from.

But after a few thousand years, the necro-evolution of machines - as in Stanislaw Lem's novel "The Invincible" and the short story collections "The Cyberiad" - went in the direction of complete independence and independence from workshops, energy sources and other things that tied them to specific places and made them unreliable. Therefore, robots in the course of necroevolution began to biologize and hybridize, thus creating different types of aliens: Greys, Nordics, robot-shaped clumsy "vaporizers" and others. A well-known Russian ufologist Geological Sciences Dr. Vladimir I. Tjurin-Avinskiy enumerated in his works almost 60 shapes of alien figures and more than 200 types of their vehicles known to us as UFOs, USOs or UOOs... - with which they haunt us on Earth. And so what? - that They - these intelligent machines - watch over us at every turn, observing us from their flying saucers - increasingly invisible to human eyes and graspable only by our instruments. And that is the solution to this mystery.

The hypothesis of "dead evolution after the Great God-Astronaut Conflict" has the advantage of explaining exactly all the anomalous phenomena that we observe every day and thus no longer notice them. It's high time to start noticing them!

***

May the Reader forgive us for a small saltus from the essential topic of TP and other meteorite sensations that have been described in chronicles. The point is that scholars describe only what they are able to study, while to solve these mysteries, you need to do more than analysis and research methods - you need first and foremost an imagination and   invention. Without this, there's nothing doing. In other words, we need mad hypotheses and a comprehensive study of what is left of our Antenats in the Sahara and in the jungles of the Amazon, under the ice of Antarctica and in the mountains of Tibet, the forests of Selva and the taiga of Siberia. Above all, the seven seals from the safes of the military and civilian information services should finally be removed. And the Vatican! And only then will our eyes be opened to the extraordinary reality that is so feared by those who rule this world with the power of fear and money...

***

History has a way of repeating itself, unless we learn from it... - wrote the famous treasure hunter, diver and American writer Clive Cussler in the 1980s. Right on. It would seem that we have three world wars and more than 200 local conflicts behind us and a Cold War that was unprecedented in the history of Mankind and that history has taught us something - after all, it is said to be magistra vitae est... - but it turns out that the exact opposite is true. Take a look at the following summary, Reader, and think globally for a moment:

US has 8720 nuclear warheads

Russia has 7235

France has 485

China has 425

Great Britain has 300

In addition to them, warheads are also possessed by: Libya, Israel, Iran, Brazil, India, Pakistan, South Africa

Are these "legal" (SIPRI data for 2000) 17,195 nuclear warheads so necessary for our life and happiness? - only a fool can give a nod here! And how many hungry people could be fed with the money drowned in nuclear and conventional armaments???... Can you call safe the saturated state of nuclear weapons and other WMD-type nasties for us, our environment and the Cosmos finally? Yes, the Cosmos too, because when space transportation becomes more expensive, there will always be some moron deranged by the power and material goods of this world, who will take into Space not scientific stations, not cosmonauts, but WMD... This is a danger that is already completely real and it would be a very serious mistake to underestimate it. Mankind has not, in fact, been able to conquer Space! And that is why we believe that the history of the Great Gods-Astronauts Conflict could repeat itself at any time! And it will repeat for sure, as long as the areas of monstrous poverty, social inequality and the ambitions of various "Fathers of the Nation", "Saviors of Humanity", "The Only Infallible" and other demented screw-ups are not eliminated... And then the mongrelized and degraded Humanity will laboriously rebuild everything ab ovo - from scratch... dolmens and menhirs reminiscing about the Golden Age of the 1990s and the early years of the 21st century, because they will be reminded of the glory days of a destroyed civilization - as in the cult novel by Walter M. Miller Jr. - "A Canticle for Leibowitz"...

We hope this never happens...

9.3. TM over Europe?

This question is most pertinent, as TM-like phenomena have also been seen over Europe. Of course, we omit here GPB and JUT, which we wrote about in previous chapters, and this is about objects that flew over our continent and were observed by many people - and resembled TPs in their behavior.

The reason for writing this subsection was the flight over Europe of some mysterious body in the evening of December 20, 1999, as reported by all significant and important radio and TV stations of Europe and the world.

On December 22, 1999 at 06:58 CET - thus with a delay of as much as 36 hours - this information was given by editor Andrzej Zalewski of Eko-Radio PR-1. The information sounded more or less like this:

Last night, at around 19:45, a luminous body with a golden tail was seen flying over Europe. The object was first seen in Narvik, and half an hour later in Malmö and Copenhagen, calculating its speed to be around 4,000km/h. The mysterious object was also observed in the English Channel as it flew over the Atlantic, where it disappeared behind clouds.

On the same day, at 08:00 GMT, Robert Leśniakiewicz got on the phone with Editor Zalewski, from whom he managed to pull out some more information about this UAP, namely - the Scandinavian Bolide (for that is the name he gave it), was first spotted over Narvik, Norway at 18:45 GMT, as it flew in a SW direction. Half an hour later, at 19:15 GMT, it was seen over

Sweden's Malmö and the Danish capital as it flew toward the English Channel, where it was observed flying over the Atlantic half an hour later - that is, somewhere around 19:45 GMT. And no one knows what happened to it, as it disappeared somewhere above the clouds over the Atlantic. The European Union media came up with a three hypotheses - according to them, it was:

1. A meteor or bolide, or -

2. The so-called "spacescrap" - i.e. an artificial satellite of the Earth, which ended its life in orbit around the Earth with a spectacular entry into the atmosphere, or...

3. ...UFO!

In an interview with Editor Zalewski, Robert added - as he and it seemed to him (the deviousness of a professional military and border guard) - a quite sensible hypothesis:

4. A Russian rocket launched from the military spaceport at Pliesetsk near Arkhangelsk, over which the Russians lost control, as a result of which it flew over the Atlantic instead of east towards Yakutia and the Pacific... - and there, somewhere over the Atlantic, it completed its life either burning up in the atmosphere or falling into its waters...

We were familiar with similar cases before, so Robert calmly assumed a priori that something like this had occurred here as well. Analysis of what occurred indicated that it could not have been a Russian rocket. The thing is that this UAP was moving at a speed that was about 4,000 km/h - that is, about 1.11 km/s or Ma 3.37. It would therefore resemble not a rocket, but some kind of high-speed aircraft - just like the US Aurora flying supersonic spy or the Russian Uragan. In fact, such aircraft are reportedly capable of traveling at an altitude of 60,000 meters at speeds as high as Ma 10 - that's nearly 3.3 km/s or 11,880 km/h - using oxygen-hydrogen rocket engines or a combined turbojet-rocket propulsion system. In the case described here, the speed of this UAP is as much as three times smaller! - and therefore it is neither Aurora nor Uragan.

A meteor? Again, no, because meteors move at higher speeds - from 6 to almost 76 km/s - not to mention the fact that meteors flying through the atmosphere have a velocity of their flight, which was not observed in the case of SB. Thus, it seems that the flight of this "thing" was corrected along the entire length of its trajectory so that the speed of its movement was constant.

As is evident from the table of meteor swarm activity, there are two radiators radiating on December 20, which lie in the northern hemisphere of the sky and are not bad to be the "fathers" of the SB, but... - their Vg are an order of magnitude higher than the SB velocity! That's not all, because the SB trajectory is neither orthodromic nor loxodromic. The trajectory of the SB indicates that in the vicinity of Copenhagen the SB made a turn of at least 45° to the west, something that no normal meteorite or bolide can do anymore, which is the nail in the coffin of the hypothesis of the SB's meteoritic origin. Even taking all possible corrections for the curvature of the planet and the possibility of a *jet stream*[109] at a high altitude.

---

[109] *Jet streams* are strong winds blowing in the stratosphere at speeds ranging from 180-220 km/h up to as high as 370 km/h. They most often occur at the boundary between the troposphere and the stratosphere. They are used to accelerate the flight of transoceanic aircraft.

Robert Leśniakiewicz immediately sprang into action and communicated by letter with Swedish ufologists Clas Svahn of Järfälla and Tora Greve of Malmö, both representing UFO-Sverige. Tora Greve was the first to respond and informed us that we were dealing here with a meteor coming from the Geminids swarm, nay! - but the Geminids beam from December 4-16 from a point with coordinates RE = 112°.3 and DEC = +32°.5 - and their maximum activity falls on December 14, the Vg is 34.4 km/s and it gives about 70 flashes per hour. Thus, it could not have been a meteor from the Geminids radiant. In addition, Tora Greve adds that it may have been the stage of a rocket launched from the US spaceport Vanderberg III AFB, but did not specify which rocket it might be about. A similar response came from Norway's UFO-Norge.

The most comprehensive answer came from Clas Svahn and it sounded with slight abbreviations like this:

As for the Scandinavian Bolide, we at UFO-Sverige have many accounts from credible witnesses and observers in southwestern Sweden. Thanks to contacts with UFO-Norge and Danish SUFOI, we have even more. They show that the Scandinavian Bolide flew straight from north to south and did not change its direction of flight towards the [English] Channel. The bolide flew somewhere over western Germany. It did not make a 45° turn over Malmö, and I think your information as to the beginning of the Scandinavian Bolide's flight is incorrect. The color and other physical characteristics of the Bolide are exactly the same as those of other meteors that have been observed in Sweden. (...)

Last December 20, we had not one object in Swedish airspace, but two. The first appeared in the morning at 06:15 GMT and it was a stage of an American Titan 2 rocket which entered Swedish airspace somewhere over Valdemarsvik, south of Stockholm, where it began glowing in the atmosphere. A few minutes later, that rocket segment exploded in the air somewhere over Östersund, which was seen by many civilians and military personnel. (...)

The correctness of this conclusion was confirmed by Mr. Allan Pickup - who is an expert on rocket flights and satellites. As you already know, the second object was a meteor that entered the atmosphere at 19:15 GMT, on the same day. (...) And indeed - superimposed on the map, the trajectories of these bodies form a line similar to the one you drew for me, but it was not one but two objects at different times observed over Sweden. (...)[110]

Everything is clear. The culprits are - as always - the despicable media, who have created a sensation around an essentially trivial event, such as the fall of a meteorite and the entry of a booster rocket into the Earth's atmosphere. The explanation is simple and does not require the slightest mental effort. Maybe for the Swedish military or scientists, because it is unconvincing to say the least, and this is because no one has explained to us a small but nasty little detail, namely - how come the editors of the Western media combined two events more than 12 hours apart in time into one!!!? This explanation by Clas Svahn is thus - unfortunately - unbelievable and unconvincing. Besides - as he stated in his interview for the British organization UFOIN in November 2000[111] - UFO-Sverige cooperates with the Swedish secret services, which

---

[110] Clas Svahn - Letter to Robert Leśniakiewicz dated March 10, 2000.

[111] Dave Baker - "Interview with Clas Svahn for UFOIN" - translated by me.

could mean that this organization is totally manipulated by them!...

Of other events, we should note the flight of a strange "meteor" on December 2, 1983. This object was seen over France, then over West Germany and East Germany, as well as over Poland, and then it flew over the territory of the USSR. It flew exactly over 52°N with a speed calculated at 6000 km/h or 1.6 km/s or Ma 5.05.[112] It was 7 lights pulsating in diapason $+4...+1^m$ and leaving behind a bright streak. In our case, the phenomenon began at 19:45 GMT.

At first it was thought that it was either a meteor or a spacescrap or some ex-satellite of Earth, but Robert soon had to verify his judgment after reading several studies of space warfare weapons and strategy, which was trendy in the 1980s, and came to the conclusion that it could simply have been an episode of a space war between American and Soviet satellites - an orbital battle fought between spy satellites and "killer" satellites. He discussed this hypothesis with one of the most prominent experts in the field - Prof. Zbigniew Schneigert (d. 1998) of Zakopane, one of the Polish members of the AAS - who took a positive stance on the matter.[113] In this view, it looked as follows: one side placed a super-spy in orbit that the opposing side did not wish to see over its territory. The opposing side sent its "killers" satellites to neutralize it. This was answered by sending "anti-killer" satellites to take care of the "killers" satellites... - As a result, after making a

---

[112] Thomas Mehner - "History of the ufology movement in East Germany" in "UFO" No. 4/1991, translated by me.

[113] Robert K. Leśniakiewicz - "UFOs over the border", Kraków 2000.

full rotation around the Earth, there was nothing left in orbit. This would have been the first of the Cold War space battles, in which the two "Star Wars"-like systems clashed???...

Another, no less intriguing interesting fact was the Greenland Meteorite, which fell to Earth on December 7 or 9, 1997 in Greenland. There would be nothing surprising about it, if it were not for the fact that the energy of this impact was about 20-25 kt TNT - as much as the energy of the "Little Boy" atomic bomb explosion that turned Hiroshima into ashes. The most interesting thing, however, is that this information was taken off the PAP world news service within 2 hours! - so that it was only reported by our "Super Express" in the pen of editor Ewa Jabłońska. Later, an article appeared in a magazine about the search for this very meteorite in Greenland, but which - supposedly - was not found. It's strange, but there should have been some trace of the impact left on the ice armor of Greenland - however, there was none, ergo either the meteorite exploded in the air, like TM, or it wasn't a meteorite at all, or it was some military satellite of the Russians, Americans or Chinese, or maybe Atlanteans?... for now, it's an "X-Files" case and there is no solution in sight.

Roman Rzepka is of the opinion that on December 9, 1997, a meteorite fell on Greenland in the vicinity of Nuuk (Godthåb), at N 64°20' and W 054°30', moving at an extraordinary speed in the atmosphere of the Earth - as much as 56 km/s. so it appears that this meteorite came from the depths... of the Galaxy! The remains of the meteorite were not found - reportedly... and this was the argument for orthodox scientists claiming that such meteorites simply do not exist... - because they have no right to penetrate deep into the Solar System. The scientist, who worked at the renowned Niels Bohr Institute in Copenhagen - Dr. Lars Lindberg Christiansen for putting out the view that it was an out-of-system meteorite, was simply fired from his job with immediate effect...

So far, the Greenland Meteorite case is open. I suspect that it has been found, and has shared the fate of all artifacts inconvenient to orthodox science, such as the "cube of Gurtl" or the "sphere of Żabno" - has been destroyed or is rotting somewhere at the bottom of the basement of the Niels Bohr Institute or some American air base...

And here is another interesting digression: at the end of the 19th century, the great Jules Verne wrote a novel entitled. "The Chase of the Golden Meteor", in which there is a huge golden meteorite worth 60,000,000,000,000,000,000,000,000 then francs - now you could multiply that by 100. This miraculous meteorite was supposed to fall on the southern edge of the island of Upernivik (Uppernavick, Upernavik) at N 72°51'30" and W 055°35'18". Could it be that this was a prophetic vision of a brilliant writer, dictated by an unusually sharp, even aquarian intuition?... Indeed, he was not much mistaken, only by a few hundred kilometers!

It goes on. On July 7, 1999, at 03:15 GMT on New Zealand, it was possible to film the fall of a meteorite the size of a passenger car, which exploded with a bang, emitting a strong flash of blue light. So, TP in miniature? No, because some debris was found...

What does all this prove? It may prove that such strange meteorites accompany the appearance of comets. In 1999-2000, we were expecting the magnificent spectacle that astronomers promised us in connection with the flyby at a distance of 0.33 AU from Earth, discovered in September 1999, of the Millennium Comet - C/1999 S4 (LINEAR) - which was supposed to be brighter than the previously observed bright comets Hayakutake and Hale-Bopp.

Its brightness was expected to be as high as -4m - the same as Venus at full. Unfortunately, the Millennium Comet turned out to be a big dud, its brightness turned out to be much lower than scientists' calculations.,[114] which quite accurately resembled the disappointment of another comet C/1973 E1 (Kohoutek). Incidentally, the next bright comet C/2001 A2 (LINEAR) is expected in July 2001 and can be observed with the naked eye in the constellations of Whale (28-30.VI.), Fish (1-10.VII.) and Pegasus (from 11.VII.), and its brightness is predicted to be > +5m - and such it was...

NB, perhaps it was the mysterious failure of the Hubble Space Telescope in mid-November 1999 that was caused by meteors from the Leonid swarm, whose maximum fell on the night of November 18/19, 1999, between 00:00 and 03:00 CET. As many as 3,000 flashes per hour were counted in Japan and other countries where the phenomenon was observed, ergo any meteor could have hit the LAT LST Edwin Hubble and damaged it so that the crew of the STS Discovery had to replace its computer, radio transmitter, data logger and six gyroscopes, and install armored meteorite shields. And here the thought comes to mind that maybe the EHST was damaged by Someone intentionally and deliberately in order to prevent it from registering something that

---

[114] Such data was presented by Prof. Dr. **K. Ziołkowski** in an interview to PR-1 on December 23, 1999.

was not meant for our eyes???... It has been known for a long time that in orbit around the Earth our satellites sometimes behave surprisingly strangely, as if an unknown Someone turns them on and off regardless of the will of their owners or disposers...

EHST wasn't the only one in trouble, as 1999 was an unlucky year for the Russians and Americans in general.

That's all that leaked into the media, and how much more information of this kind was withheld on this occasion, only God knows... Editor Andrzej Zalewski rightly pointed out that either the American space probes are done "the Polish way", i.e., poorly and don't work as they should, or - what's even worse - the Ufo simply... eliminate them! This is especially true for Mars, because out of 32 interplanetary probe missions, only 8 were successful! The remaining 75% of Earth's spacecraft stopped working near the Red Planet! And this was at a time when two transpluto probes, Pioneer 10 and Pioneer 11, had already moved 10 billion kilometers away from Earth and gone beyond the Solar System - heading for the constellation of Taurus.

On January 19, 2000, the Americans conducted an unsuccessful test of a new anti-missile over the Pacific Ocean. This was another step toward the creation of a space-based shield of the SDI/NMD system.

On February 10, 2000, Japan's NASDA[115] screwed up with the Astro E satellite, with which communications were suddenly lost from the NASDA Communications Center in Kagoshima. There is a possibility that this satellite was hit by some sort of ice ball,

---

[115] Japan's National Astronautical Agency, today JAXA.

which bombed Belgium on January 12 this year, Toledo area in Spain on January 20, Treviso area in Italy on January 25, and on January 27 ice blocks fell on Milan, Treviso, Bologna, Venice and other cities in northern and central Italy...

In late 2000, the Russians had a serious problem with the Mir space station. On December 25 at 15:00 Moscow time, all radio communications with Mir's automation broke down. All attempts to restore it burned to the ground. Mir was silent and deaf to all signals from the Space Flight Center of the Russian Cosmonautics Agency... Of course, speculation began about where the 15-year-old 140-ton space station would fall, and controversial fashion designer Paco Rabane announced that Mir would fall on Paris. Fortunately, and to the incredible astonishment of Mir's ground crew, the station's automatics responded at 3 p.m. Moscow time on December 26 as if nothing had ever... What happened aboard Mir during those 24 hours, no one knows, while we were intrigued by the fact of the unexpected change of Mir's crew, which was changed in emergency mode the very next day! Could it be that not a cosmonaut was sent there, but someone with a completely different specialty and by no means an IT or communications specialist? Someone from the Aerospace Forces of the Russian Federation?...

But this is not the end of Russian failures, because on December 28, 2000, a Cyclone 3 rocket with six military and commercial satellites on board fell into the Barents Sea! That is, it was presumed that this rocket fell there, because meanwhile, it was reported from eastern Australia that six meteors were seen there and burned up in the Earth's atmosphere. Perhaps these were precisely the "missing" satellites from Cyclone 3...

And another thing - on July 20, 2001, the Russians carried out a strange experiment codenamed "Volna"[116], which consisted in launching a missile aboard a submarine in the Barents Sea, its suborbital flight over Russia and landing in Kamchatka. There would be nothing interesting about it, if it were not for the fact that the experiment was aimed at... to try out a new propulsion system - the so-called "solar sail" - for spacecraft. I'm afraid this is a curve ball, and it's about an experimental flight of a anti-missile in response to an analogous U.S. experiment that took place about a week earlier - on July 13, when an anti-missile launched from Kualajainen Atoll destroyed a Minuteman-class ICBM launched from the military spaceport at Vanderburg III AFB in California. I wonder if this involved shooting down an enemy ICBM, or something else?... - for example, a large meteorite or an alien spacecraft? The most interesting thing is that information about this experiment disappeared from all services of all agencies - exactly like the Greenland Meteorite!... To make things even more interesting, the next day after this experiment, masses of water collapsed on southern Poland and another Megaflood began - of identical strength to the one that ravaged Lower Silesia in July 1997... Tomasz Niesporek, a well-known ufologist from Katowice, MA, even came up with the conjecture that this flood was the result of the Russian version of the American HAARP program, that notorious ELIPTON, with which the Kremlin "hawks" scare us - as indicated by the very codename of the experiment - "Wave". Perhaps it was an experiment with high-frequency radio

---

[116] Wave.

waves that would be capable of destroying the warheads of US ICBMs flying at Mother Russia!...

As you can see from the above, something bad is happening in the immediate space vicinity of Earth, and this something worries us - ufologists - because it is one more proof that They are watching us and that the observation phase of Contact is coming to an end!

This is evidenced by strange crop circles and pictograms found here and there, which sometimes give us information from the future. The problem is that we don't want to read them because we are afraid to speak out about them. For there are religious brakes, as evidenced by the work of Józef Grzywok of the Movement of Supporters of the Existence of Aliens, stemming mainly from the fact that the Catholic Church and other churches treat aliens mainly as... competition for cash! On the other hand, governments and official science, with the stubbornness and cheek of mafiosos, are going not to give up and pushing us that aliens do not exist at all, although, on the other hand, it is common knowledge that all secret services of all countries - from Albania to Zimbabwe - and from the American CIA and Israeli Mossad to the Russian SWR have spec cells studying UAPs, their activities on Earth and beyond... That's why substitute problems like Problem 9999 or Problem Y2K are invented, to create a curve ball for these research programs. That's exactly right!

We are under the vague impression that there are certain forces at work: an unknown Someone or Something is deliberately keeping us - the world community - in ignorance and thus in check, according to the principle "knowledge = power" and preventing us from achieving a higher knowledge of the

Cosmos and the laws governing it. The failures of our space missions are concrete and tangible proof of this - and irresistible proof!

Let's not be crazy about scientists, priests and politicians, because both some, the others and the third want to hold on to the manger and the trough as long as possible, so let's do our job - the moon doesn't care for barking dogs...

9.4. May Polish Bolides?

This story took place on May 6, 2000 between the hours of 13:00 and 14:00 CEST (11:00 and 12:00 GMT) - in southern Poland. At that time, many witnesses observed the flight of a strange object, glowing with a strong light, which showed itself to the north and flew south.

Bronisław Rzepecki was one of the first ufologists to receive a report of the sighting of this body from his neighbor from Paryż near Krzeszowice (Lesser Poland Voivodeship), who observed this UFO between 13:50 and 14:00. And here is her report:

It looked like a dark gray triangle, slightly smaller than the full moon, and had clearly defined outlines and rounded tops. Streaks emanated from the back of the object and were white, yellow and red in color. The longest was the central streak - white - about 5 times longer than the triangle and located vertically behind the object - vide the figure. The other two were shorter - about 3 times the length of the triangle and departed at a certain angle to the main streak. The object flew very fast - the observation lasted 3-4 seconds and quite silently.

These observations were confirmed from an unexpected angle by editor Robert Bernatowicz of "Nautilius Radia Zet", who quoted a witness from Wojsławice near Niemcza, where on May 6, 2000, a sphere was seen followed by a streak. It was flying very fast from west to east!

Another telephone call reported the fact of the flight in the vicinity of Kaczenice near Zielona Góra and Wałbrzych of a sphere with a tail, which this time moved slowly... And at the same time, a shooting star was seen in Kielce at 14:00, flying from north to south.

On May 6, 2000, between the hours of 13:00 and 14:00, a number of residents of Osielec (Sucha Beskidzka district, Lesser Poland voivodeship), observed a luminous flying object on the western side of the sky. The object was in the shape of a sphere and trailed behind it a flame tail with a length of 3 diameters of that sphere. The UFO was also visible in Jordanów, where it was observed by students of the Agricultural Technical School in Chrobaczym.

This UAP emitted a strong white-yellow light, which the youngest witnesses of the event also described as "rainbow". The entire flyby took place in absolute silence, and everything pointed to the fact that it was a sighting of a Daily Object!!!...

On May 15 and 17, 2000, Robert Leśniakiewicz, together with Dr. Stanisław Buda, conducted an investigation for the CBZA, the results of which, however, suggested that this UFO was only a rare phenomenon of a meteorite flying through the Earth's atmosphere. The meteorite entered the Earth's atmosphere somewhere over the central stretches of Poland and exploded over Jablunkov in the Czech Republic at an altitude of about 20,000 meters - while its remains also fell on our Cieszyn Silesia. Andrzej Kotowiecki, M.A., is searching for them. Everyone linked this event to the close flyby of comet C/1999 S4 (LINEAR), which caused such a disappointment to sky observers!... They notified the Institute of Astronomy of the University of Wrocław of the observations made.[117]

Meanwhile, the already mentioned here editor Bernatowicz has received nearly 20 reports of sightings of this "meteorite" from the vicinity of Bielsko-Biała, Krzeczyn Wielki (near Lubin, Lower Silesia province), Międzybrodzie Bialskie, Wrocław, Górki Wielkie and other locations. Thus, it seems that not one, but two bolides were seen: the first flying from west to east and the second flying from north to south - well, unless we accept as true that this bolide made a 90° turn to the south! The second matter of controversy is the shape of this UFO - once a sphere with a tail, once a triangle with tails - and as many as three! Isn't this reminiscent of the controversy built up over the trajectories and shapes of TMs? So it was not a bolide of any kind - as authoritatively stated Dr. Paweł Preś of IAUW - but a "real" UFO - TRUFO!

But the sensations didn't end there, because almost three weeks later - on May 30, 2000, at about 21:10, a bizarre incident occurred over Morask near Poznań (actually, it's already a district

---

[117] In the case of observation of a meteorite fall, notify the Institute of Astronomy of the University of Wrocław, ul. Kopernika 11, 51-622 Wrocław.

of Poznań). At about that hour, a dozen people saw something they associated with a sport avionet flying toward the ground smoking thickly, as if it were on fire. Several people heard a loud bang, so they concluded that the plane had crashed to the ground. A search operation was launched and - not even a trace of the crashed plane was found. The plane - a specter! What was it? - no one knows. The case resembles a typical Moscow circus - there was something and there isn't, and like in a Czech movie - nobody knows anything... If it was a meteorite, an impact crater would have to be found by the way. Such was not found there, ergo it was not a meteorite impact - well, what then?[118]

In conclusion, let me, the Reader, cite a list of meteorites and other objects that may (but absolutely not necessarily) be meteorites, which fell on the territory of our country and were found here. One thing is certain - TM was not the only puzzling object that fell to Earth and thus caused a lot of confusion. TP was just one of the largest and caused the most damage. And that's why it works on our imagination the most.

And a few more words about the last item in the table, an event that played out literally within days. Well, on June 30, 2001, at 05:30 CEST (03:30 GMT), in the forest on the western slope of the mountain Luboń Wielki - 1022 m above sea level - slightly below the hamlet of Krzysie (Surówki) - fell a 6 kg meteorite, which was composed not of stone, coal or metal, but of deeply frozen... brine! Its unusual appearance and color drew the attention of a witness to its fall - 19-year-old Andrzej Bednarczyk

---

[118] A detailed description of the events mentioned here will be found by the Reader in "Czas UFO" No. 4/2000.

from Skomielna Biała, who saw its fall preceded by a booming swish, like a jet flying low over the ground. The fact that the witness first heard the swish and then saw the meteorite fall cutting spruce branches along the way proves that this chunk of brine - with a beautiful apricot color and the smell of sea salt - was moving at a speed of < 1 Ma. The fact that the meteorite had a slightly frothy salty taste indicates, according to the ruling of Prof. Bogdan Rompolt of the Institute of Astronomy at the University of Wrocław, that we are dealing here with a fragment of the head (or rather, nucleus) of a comet.

Although after analysis at the IAUW it turned out that this was just a so-called salt lick for animals, still no one has answered the basic question: what was this body, which fell into the woods on the slope of Luboń Wielki, and which probably still lies there - if it was a meteorite and not some man-made or alien structure?...

This would then mean that the TP mystery has been solved? Not at all. This is just one point in support of the validity of the hypothesis that on June 30, 1908, the Earth was struck by the head of a comet that caused such terrible havoc. Now, in 2001, the Earth was hit only by some splinter that fell off the nucleus of the TP and orbited for 93 years before not falling to Earth. A closer study of the Skomielna Biała Meteorite should shed new light on this age-old problem of the Tunguska Unusual Thing...[119]

---

[119] Most likely, this "meteorite" was not a meteorite, but... a lick of Kłodawa salt intended for animals! Nevertheless, the question remains open, what did the witness actually hear and see on that critical day in the forest near Luboń Wielki? We suspect that the thing that fell then is still lying there and waiting for its discoverer... Personally, I am of the opinion that we are dealing with two objects: a lick and a so-called megacriometeorite, which fell and

shattered into fragments,. Which melted and seeped into the ground. A witness in search of the meteorite came across the brine and assumed it was the meteorite - if only because of the shape and color of it.

10. M. Jesenský - LIFE ON THE MOON?

And now it's going to be really interesting, because I present the Reader with Dr. Miloš Jesenský's paper for the Eighth Central European Ufological Congress in Košice in 1999. It is interesting because the Author, while writing it, used only popular-scientific and publicly available sources, but he had to pick out this information like gems in the various junk and gibberish flooding us with the ocean of information media and disinformation from the "only right" science. And here is what the Author has to tell us:

***

Galileo di Vincenzo Bonaiuti de' Galilei, known by the Latinized name of Galileo Galilei, at the age of 45, learned in June 1609 during his stay in Venice that a lenticular telescope had been built in the Netherlands, with which it was possible to zoom in and magnify objects under study. He soon began to grind the glasses himself and put them together in such a way that he perfected it to such an extent that from a three-fold magnification he obtained as much as a thirty-fold magnification.

And so it came to pass that the famous scientist, who was at the University of Padua at the time, turned his telescope toward the starry sky, thus making his mark in human history as the first scientist to begin the era of instrumental studies of the celestial spheres. He then pointed the telescope at the Moon, and...

Moon... - the eye of the Renaissance scholar was captivated by the sight of the vast panorama of the Silver Globe's surface: mountains that cast sharp shadows; craters, valleys and seas. At the same time, the dark side of the Moon shone with a faint glow, as if a light reflected from the Earth. Thus, against all the accusations that the fathers of the Catholic Church threw in the face of Nicolaus Copernicus, he already had more than the learned canon from Frombork - the evidence was right in front of him!

"What a marvelous invention this is, which allows us to approximate the lunar body distant from the Earth by 60 of its diameters to only two Earth diameters," wrote Galileo Galilei in his treatise "Sidericus nuncius" published in 1610, "And thanks to which it can be definitively ruled that the Moon does not have a smooth mirror-like surface, but has an undulating one, and is like the Earth covered with mountains, deep valleys and ridges.

Repeated observations have brought us to the conclusion, Galileo Galilei writes elsewhere, that the Moon's surface is not homogeneous and flat, and its body perfectly spherical - as many thinkers presumed - but it is uneven and, like the Earth's surface, is covered with mountains and valleys.

Galileo also added to his observations a drawing depicting the Moon on the 20th day after the new moon, on which one can see such formations as Mare Serenitatis, Mare Nubium, Mare Humorum, the western part of Oceanus Procellarum, Sinus Roris,

Mare Frigoris, Mare Imbrium and the craters Copernicus and Ptolmeus, which, however, are marked rather inaccurately.

Galileo's remarks in "Sidericus nuntius" are material that mixes the volatility of a visionary with sound science and a scientist's admiration for the enormous strides that knowledge has made. His contemporaries considered most interesting the discovery that the vast majority of lunar mountains are circular in shape. Their uniqueness brought some scholars - such as the German astronomer Johannes Kepler (1571-1630) to the conclusion that these mountains are artificial creations - probably fortified walls of Lunar cities.[120]

In the same way, the characters in Jules Verne's (1828-1905) famous novel "Around the Moon" (1870) during their circumlunar flight in a hollowed-out artillery shell, admired the cleverness of the Moon's inhabitants, who located their city in the crater of Tycho:

There is nothing as powerful as these defensive walls, which provide security for the residents of this city. This city would be unconquered. Travelers admired the towers and mountains as works of lunar construction. On one site could stand a church, and there a citadel...

Could it be that Verne predicted what we are now discovering with automated lunar probes and manned expeditions to the moon?...[121]

---

[120] J. Kepler - „Somnium seu astronomia lunaris", Tübingen 1609.
[121] Also our countryman Jerzy Żuławski described life on the Moon writing "Na Srebrnym Globie" (Kraków, 1909 2nd ed.: Kraków 1979)!

10.1. After Galileo

Our brave travelers developed in their profound reflections the view of the great 19th century astronomer Franz von Gruithuisen (1774-1852), who believed that the Moon was inhabited. He was a persistent observer of the Silver Globe, who gave names to two lunar mountains and a crater near the Mairan crater, and in his work presented a drawing of fortresses and buildings of the Selenites[122], as he saw them through his telescope, and so described them in his own book:

These creatures live like our fish, but at the bottom of caves and deep crevices, or like our earthworms and moles... Perhaps in these depths they build their strongholds and cities, that is, completely in a more opaque way than with us. After all, our underground Rome is bigger than the one we see every day... Do we have any grounds to claim that people on the Moon are less hardworking than ants?

Today his remarks seem grotesque to us, to say the least, but...

At a time when the conquest of the Moon has become a fact, it would not be out of place to mention some of the strange events on our natural satellite, which cause us to ask whether the Moon has not already once served as a base for creatures from another world, which creatures wanted to get to know us better and study our civilization... - wrote well-known science columnist and writer George Langelaan in his commentary for the magazine

---

[122] Alleged inhabitants of the moon.

"Planéte", published in five languages. He called himself a "chronicler of cursed events" that blandly do not fit the image produced by modern science. [...][123]

10.2. Strange event in Linnaeus crater

In 1866, selenographer Johann Schmidt published information that the small crater Linné or Linnaeus, located in the eastern part of the Sea of Brightness at a position described by the selenographic coordinates N 27°,7 and E 11°,8, which in 1823 he observed with Wilhelm G. Lohrmann (1796-1840) and Johann H. von Mädler (1794-1874), being a rather deep crater casting sharp shadows at low Sun, now looked like a white spot with an invisible bottom. Linnaeus Crater still has this appearance today...

Schmidt's discovery is interesting in that it may not have been Linnaeus' crater, but another one, however, Lohrmann and Mädler knew its exact location - nay! - they used it as a landmark and starting point in their selenographic measurements! The most interesting thing, however, is that the whitish surrounding of this crater shows... periodic changes that the American astronomer Edward Ch. Pickering (1846-1919) also observed in other places on the Moon's surface, including a spot east of the central hill of Eratosthenes crater - at N 14°.5 and W 11°.3. Here one can observe a whitish spot of 24 x 13 km, which just after sunrise

---

[123] I have omitted descriptions of lunar topography and explanations of nomenclature here, which I give the reader in Polish.

begins to diminish and at noon completely disappears, and then shows itself again at dawn. Pickering explained this phenomenon by the fact that water evaporates there during the lunar day, which settles there at night in the form of frost - which would be proof directly of the presence of water on the Moon!

Unfortunately, the latest *Lunar Prospector* probe mission has shown that there is no water on the Moon[124], but this, of course, does not constitute any evidence, because Lunar Prospector may have hit not a water-bearing area in the perpetual lunar shadow, but a dike or other "dry" place of the crater. Perhaps water exists on the Moon, but bound to rock, such as in concrete. Such rock would make excellent building material, but the water not contained in them would not be detectable to the lunar probe apparatus... Anyway, the question of the presence of water on the Moon is still open despite the fact that the Moon has an incredibly rarefied atmosphere - its density is about 10-13 of what we have on Earth - so it is a vacuum more perfect than what we manage to obtain in our laboratories on Earth. Under the conditions of this high vacuum and a temperature diapason of +110°C to -150°C, water must vaporize into space - a certainty! But then why are there no traces of water in the Moon's atmosphere composed mainly of argon (Ar), carbon dioxide (CO_2) and chad (CO)?

The *Lunar Prospector* probe had a "neutron nose" to pick up the neutron flux from the Moon and measure its intensity - where it was high, water was not to be expected, while where it was low,

---

[124] Of course, in a liquid state, because the **Lunar Prospector** probe made the discovery of water ice in both polar regions of the Moon! (according to "Encyklopedia Multimedialna pwn.pl")

water could be found in solid or liquid or gas (water vapor). The maps show the area around the North Pole, where the most water-bearing areas are circled in blue. But let's return to other lunar mysteries.

The next case of an obvious and strange change on the surface of the Silver Globe is a pair of craters lying on the plane of the Sea of Fertility - the 9 x 11 km oval Messier crater, located at S 1°.9 and E 47°.6, and the twin 13 x 11 km Messier A crater, from which two bright rays diverge to the west. German selenographers Wilhelm Beer (1797-1850) and Johann Mädler described them as equal in diameter, which now have completely unequal dimensions.[125]

On May 19, 1877, astronomer Hermann J. Klein (1844-1914) discovered near the crater Hyginus - N 7°.8 and E 6°.3, in a land repeatedly described, photographed, searched, mapped and cataloged - as one commentator wrote - a new crater: Hyginus N. On October 14, 1891, Ladislav Weinek (1848-1913), director of Prague's Klementina Astronomical Observatory and author of an atlas of the Moon, discovered a new crater in the vicinity of the craters Billy - S 13°.8 and W 50°.1 - and Hansten - S 11°.5 and W 52° - which had never been seen in this area. In 1910, English selenographer Walter Goodacre (1856-1938) discovered three small craters in the southern part of the Solstice (Crisis) Sea using

---

[125] There was a theory explaining this phenomenon: a long time ago, a meteorite flying almost at a tangent hit the site of the Messier craters, and it shot through the lunar soil, creating these craters and the streaks that departed from them. Today this is not so certain, for all indications are that Messier A crater is an inlet crater, while Messier is an outlet crater!...

a refractor with a 263-mm objective diameter, while using a 300-mm refractor he found five more new craters and a number of bright spots on the Moon's disk.

Let's go back to the beginning of the history of noteworthy events on the Moon. On May 3, 1715, French astronomer Joseph Liouville at 09:30 observed flashes of light rays on the western edge of the Moon's disk. These flashes were irregular and always came out of the unlit side. Johann H. Schröter saw a bright light flying through the Sea of Rain on October 12, 1875. The glowing spot glided in a straight line toward the north, while a similar phenomenon was also observed in the south.[126]

There is another mystery associated with Schröter's name - in the second half of the 18th century he observed an area west of the Solstice Sea, where he discovered a new crater and named it Alhazen a.k.a. Abu Ali al-Hassan (987-1038), whose diameter was 23 miles, or about 37 km, with a gray-colored bottom. A German selenographer assured that this crater was perfectly visible and its appearance changed over time. In 1825, another German - Georg F. K. Kunowsky ((1776-1846) announced that he could not find the crater where Schröter had seen it, and that it had simply... disappeared! Alhazen at that time could not be found even by the great Mädler himself, who finally transferred the name Alhazen on his map of the Moon - the famous "Mappa Selenographica" - to another crater with a sharply outlined shaft, 33 km in diameter and coordinates: N 15°,9 and E 71°,8.

---

[126] Similar things were also observed on Mars, see St. R. Brzostkiewicz - "Czerwona planeta", Warsaw 1976.

Shortly afterwards, the discoverer of the asteroid 3 Juno - Karl L. Harding (1765-1834) spoke up, suspecting that the crater undergoes periodic changes and is sometimes not visible at all. This conjecture was confirmed in 1828 by another German - Kohler, who discovered that Schröter's crater was in fact a hillock marked on Beer and Mädler's map with the Greek letter alpha (α).

What is interesting - the metamorphosis of this piece was still going on - according to Kohler, it was not a crater at all, but an elliptical valley contained between the hills and a visible opening towards the nearby Solstice Sea. Three decades later - in 1862 - Alhazen Crater was attempted to be found by English astronomer William R. Birt (1804-1881), who found low and round mountains in the vicinity of Beer's and Maedler's "object α" - which matched Schroeter's description of Alhazen. What was happening in the land on the western coast of the Solstice Sea has not been explained to this day...

The Alhazen problem is not the only example of strange and mysterious processes on the Moon's surface. On the shore of the Sea of Frosts, near the crater Fontanelle - N 63°,4 and W 18°,9 - there is a strange formation, consisting of many somehow scattered cubes, resembling ruins. Even Julius Verne wrote about them in his novel "Around the Moon." A curious and mysterious thing, because on the maps of such experienced observers of the Moon as Beer, Mädler and Neison, there is a regular quadrangle in this place, which looked quite like an artificial construction, and in older literature it is mentioned as Maedler's Square - Mädler's Square. When in 1950 J. J. Martlett announced that Mädler's Square no longer existed, we are left to ask: what forces caused the change in this part of the Moon that led to the destruction of this regular square-shaped formation?

In addition to the changes mentioned here, there is a whole series of unexplained short-term phenomena on the surface of our natural satellite, which are simply referred to as "lunar events". Their existence began with the discovery made by Russian astronomer N. A. Kozyrev, who observed a strange cloud over the central hill of Alphonse crater - S 13°.4 and W 2°.8 - for 120 minutes, on November 3, 1958, from 01:00 GMT. This cloud made the crater's central mountain invisible, while the crater itself had a red tint. The spectroscope indicated that there were lines of carbon dioxide... Since there is no evidence of lunar volcanic activity, this would mean that there was an artificially induced... chemical explosion! So we are not surprised that the Americans directed their Ranger 9 probe there, which crashed in the NE part of the crater in March 1965...

Kozyrev was lucky - or maybe he knew what to look for - and three years later, in November and December 1961 - the same phenomenon was observed by him in the vicinity of Aristarchus crater - N 27°.7 and W 47°.4 - and was it just a coincidence that in 1966 the Soviet probe *Luna 13* landed there???... NB, this lunar land is known for the appearance of many "lunar events", and so: on October 29, 1963, astronomers J. I. Greenacre and E. Barr saw three glowing red spots in the interior of Aristarchus crater, which at one point abruptly disappeared. But already on November 24 of the same year, more observers saw on the slope of this crater at a time of more than an hour, a distinct red spot, the existence of which had to be believed and admitted by the staunchest skeptics!... This is not a modern phenomenon, as red spots in this crater were already observed by Polish astronomer and selenographer Jan Hevelius (1611-1687) and the famous Friederick William Herschell (1738-1822), who observed an explosion in the crater on the night of April 19/20. Other "lunar events" have been reported before at the crater-phantom Pitatus - S 29°.8 and W 13°.5 - in the eastern Sea of Clouds. Strange luminous phenomena were also seen near the partially destroyed crater Heracleitus - S 49°.2 and E 6°.2 - on the rampart rim of the crater Plato - N 51°.6 and E 9°.3 - and at the bottom of the Alpine Valley (Transverse Valley) formation - N 49°.0 and E 3°.0.

Information about them caused selenographers F.J. Flamm and E.F. Lingenfelter to meticulously analyze all observations of the Moon in 1965 with special attention to "lunar events." The result of this was surprising - in the area of Aristarchus crater alone, 19 instances of red spots were seen between 1783 and 1963, with 16 of them appearing on the shadowed side!

Further information about mysterious lights on the Moon was compiled by employees of the observatory in Pulsnitz, Saxony, Germany, in 1969, and they speak of at least 500 sightings in different centuries. As for Aristarchus crater, as many as 27 cases of "luminous eruptions" were recorded there between June 1963 and October 1966 alone. In January 1968, as many as 140 were recorded!

"In no other part of the Moon have so many eruptions been observed", writes the German scientists in the information, where in addition to the phenomena in Aristarchus crater we also find a description of 42 flashes in Plato crater and further: "Alphonse, Gassendi and Tycho with 13 eruptions..."

Prof. Patrick Moore conducted a detailed analysis of these phenomena, called "moonblinks" in English-language nomenclature, and covered them with a comprehensive term - *Transient Lunar Phenomena* - Short-Term Lunar Phenomena - hereafter TLP. And this is how he wrote about them:

There are too many facts in favor of the existence of TLPs, not to mention Kozyrev's observations in Alphonse crater, where he saw red clouds in 1958, however, we know very little about them. Contrary to many theories, we know nothing about their origin and occurrence...

However, there are terrain formations such as Aristarchus, Alphonse and Gassendi where TLPs occur most frequently, and these are the areas that should be covered as closely as possible...

Not to be groundless, Prof. Moore compiled the TLP catalog, which contained about 700 items![127]

One of the last TLP sightings on the Moon, according to our information, dates to May 23, 1985, when a Greek observer managed to photograph a flash of light on the surface of the Silver Globe. Personally, I think that the strange play of signals from the lunar land will continue even in the years beyond the threshold of the third millennium, and we stand on the threshold of learning something that until recently was unthinkable by most specialists - it is about traces of life on the Moon!!!

---

[127] P. Moore - "Chronological Catalogue of Events on the Moon," New York 1968.

10.3. Life on the Silver Globe?

Before we consider the possibility of organic life on the Moon, let's try to take a closer look at the issue of the presence of water on Earth's faithful satellite.

A well-known dogma says that the Moon has no atmosphere, ergo no liquid can exist on its surface. Contrary to this, in the history of selenology there were researchers who were convinced that the effects of water are still observed on its surface today. Thus, in the early 1860s, Czech geologist K. Žebera put forward the idea that long ago the Moon's surface must have been covered by water, which flushed loose mineral fractions from the polar regions and sedimented them in the lowlands - in the lunar seas. Žebera gave a concrete example of the manifestation of water erosion - the Schröter Valley - N 1°,0 and W 6°,0 - a 40 km long furrow, which, according to him, was washed out by flowing water.

Like K. Žebera, S.J. Peale believes that this *Rima Schroeter* and other sinuous furrows were created on the Moon by moving masses of not very viscous liquid across its surface - that is, most likely, water... Nay! What's more - Peale claims that this water exists to this day on the Moon and is trapped under a layer of permafrost, about 1 km thick. In this view, it would be a slowly evaporating frozen swamp, covered by a hundred-meter, or perhaps even a kilometer, layer of fine lunar regolith, which provides excellent thermal insulation![128] This hypothesis is

---

[128] Let me remind everyone that the thermal conductivity of lunar rocks is

supported by the fact that sinuous furrows are found only in the vicinity of sea basins, while never on continents! And this would mean that water and other liquid chemical compounds could (and still can) be found around the sea basins of the Silver Globe...

Undoubtedly, it would be a fascinating discovery in the future to confirm J.J. Gilvary's old hypothesis from the early 1960s, according to which the lunar seas are de facto remnants of the formerly sediment-covered seas, and that life existed in these seas, which, after the seas dried up, colored the sediments a darker color.[129]

The incidence of water vapor on the Moon was mapped by author Rosemary E. Guiley in her article for the Mond Almanac, in which she cited descriptions of past observations, as well as the work of another astronomer dating back to 1932:

A white spot appeared and expanded for one minute in the NE direction until it reached the edge of the crater. This observation was made by my friend, who could not believe his eyes. The spot continued to move until it formed something like a cloud.

According to Rosemary Guiley, a similar incident was recorded in 1958 by two amateur astronomers:

---

about 1,000 times lower than the rocks on Earth!

[129] This hypothesis also explains the presence of mascons under the lunar seas. The factor causing the increase of the gravitational field could be precisely sediments, whose density and therefore also mass would be greater than the density of the surrounding sea terrain, hence the concentration of mass at the bottom of the seas, and therefore the positive gravitational anomaly, which agrees with the observed facts...

We once observed the Moon's surface near Alphonse crater. At one point, a large opaque cloud obscured the interior of the crater. The cloud was about 20 miles/37 km and irregular in shape. Two things attracted our attention: the cloud was huge compared to the central mountain, which it covered completely, and there was a spray of light coming out of it...

These and other observations have in the past given fuel to speculation about the lunar biosphere on more than one occasion. Some researchers, such as American scientist Edward Ch. Pickering, at the beginning of the last century presumed that there was some primitive vegetation on the Moon after all, on the level of our lichens.[130] They supported their claims with multiple observations of the temporal darkening of the bottoms of certain craters and sea surfaces, which were tum darker the higher the sun stood above the local horizon.[131] Pickering gave a characteristic example of such darkening - a dark spot in the circle of the Eratosthenes crater - N 14°.5 and W 11°.3 - which terminates the chain of the lunar Apennine to the southwest. The de facto spot is made up of many smaller ones that merge into one, and during the lunation it changes its color exactly as one would expect from a carpet of lichen.[132]

---

[130] Lichens are organisms that are hybrids of fungi and green plants that are optimally adapted to any extreme environmental conditions.

[131] The aforementioned fact served **H.G. Wells** as the canvass for his novel "First Men in the Moon."

[132] Such a temporary atmosphere would have to be of low density, and during daylight hours, when the ground temperature reaches +110°C at the solar point, such a quasi-atmosphere would have to evaporate quickly. The same, by the way, is happening on Mars, where such seasonal pseudo-changes of

The American specialist goes on to point out the existence of so-called radial bands, dark stripes running out from the centers of some craters. Perhaps these are some invisible fissures in the surface of the Silver Globe, from which water vapor and carbon oxides escape, which may create a local atmosphere in which plant organisms can exist...

In the 1950s, Pickering's views were revived thanks to British professor Patrick Moore, who found that various gases come out of the fissures near the craters Aristillus - N 33°.9 and E 1°.2; Endymion - N 53°.6 and E 56°.5; Eratosthenes and Aristarchus, which allow vegetation to occur, but what it might look like - we can only guess... So, this researcher thinks, there may be some life at the bottom of deep fissures and caves below the Moon's surface, where there are more bearable temperatures and some sort of denser atmosphere.

Unfortunately, the manned expeditions did not bring back to Earth any "lunar lichen spores" between 1969 and 1972. in spite of this, scientists still hope to discover lunar life, and thanks to this, the astronauts and their equipment and soil samples were severely quarantined, because it was feared that lunar or spaceborne microorganisms would be brought to Earth.[133] Although none were detected [134] a sample of 50 g of lunar rocks was crushed and

---

the local "vegetation" have been observed.

[133] In one of his "Lunar Essays," Dr. Jesenskÿ states outright that the AIDS pandemic may have been caused by an American or Soviet unsterilized lunar probe that fell near Lake Victoria (Sese Island), and there the first infections occurred, which then spread throughout the world.

[134] Which does not mean at all that these samples were sterile, as there may have been viruses that fell to the lunar surface from cometary atmospheres,

then incubated in atmospheres consisting of different proportions of oxygen, nitrogen and carbon dioxide. There were as many as 300 samples that were incubated at temperatures of: 10, 20, 35 and 55°C, with zero results - no microorganisms were detected.

In a few cases, circular formations were spotted in the samples, which deceptively resembled bacterial colonies, however, their close analysis showed that they consisted of inorganic compounds - mainly iron. They appeared during the first four days of the experiment, then no longer.

The next microbiological study involved a sample of lunar soil from the Sea of Tranquility and the Ocean of Storms subjected to an atmosphere composed of nitrogen and carbon dioxide at temperatures of 4 and 55°C and in the presence of agate gel. After three weeks, G. Taylor found nothing.

They looked for fossilized microorganisms in samples from the Sea of Tranquility and the Ocean of Storms. The result of this study was exceedingly interesting: spherical or ellipsoidal elements were found in a thin layer of regolith - up to 10 μm - similar to vitrified rock, or fossilized microorganisms!... According to the research and estimates of D. Müller, in 1 gram of regolith there are 5×10^6 such elements, ranging in size from 0.1 to 500 μm, containing, among other things, iron, calcium, aluminum, titanium and, most interestingly, zirconium! This is not insignificant, as something similar was found in carbonaceous chondrites by Soviet scientists in 1964.

---

and were not sought by researchers who thought they simply weren't there...

It became a sensation in November 1969 when the *Apollo 12* crew brought back from the Moon the dismantled parts of the *Surveyor 3* probe, which made a soft landing in the Ocean of Storms on April 20, 1967, off the southern shores of the Island Sea. Inside the TV camera, a specimen of a living bacterium *Streptococcus mitis*[135] was found, which got there while still on Earth and survived there for two and a half years under the extreme conditions of the Silver Globe!

In his experiments, Dr. Taylor tested the toxicity of lunar soil samples, brought back by the *Apollo 11-17* expeditions, to Earth microbes. Among others, microbes of the species Pseudomonas aeroginosa, Staphylococcus aureus, as well as yeasts of the species Saccharomyces cerevisiae or Candida albicans were tested, and in only one case were samples No. 10.004 and 10.005 from the Sea of Tranquility found to be toxic to P. aeroginosa colonies. In addition, the suitability of lunar soil samples for the growth of higher plants was tested - among others, bean, grain beans, pine, etc. it turned out that lunar regolith is remarkably fertile and plants grew on it much better than on soil from Earth and with much greater intensity!

We will not go further into whether there are microorganisms on the Moon, and will now turn to looking for the answer to the question of its rational inhabitants, who may have built their bases on it, as mentioned here George Langelaan assumes.

The first report of a strange structure observed in the Solstice Sea area came on July 29, 1953, when New York Herald science

---

[135] According to other sources, it was E. coli bacteria on the outer casing of the TV camera.

editor John O'Neill, working at his observatory, could not believe his eyes. Using a 90x telescope, he matured on the empty and flat bottom of the Sea of Crises the shadow of a huge bridge more than 18 km long! O'Neill switched to 250x magnification and the huge structure appeared quite clearly in the telescope's eyepiece. The object could not be of natural origin, but only an artificial structure, and one built in record time - this part of the Moon was viewed by O'Neill five weeks ago.

O'Neill was fully aware of what he was exposing himself to by publishing such a sensation, but he wrote a memo to the "Society of Observers of Planets and the Moon," and while he belatedly wrote that "...this bridge is of natural origin...", he immediately became a thorn in the side of a whole pack of scientists," as Langelaan wrote about it.

Unexpectedly, the existence of the "O'Neill Bridge" was confirmed by Dr. Wilkins and independently by Prof. Moore, who observed it for several hours.

Dr. Wilkins in an interview with BBC radio said:

This is indeed a bridge of some sort! It measures about 12 miles long and is suspended 1,500 feet above the plane of the Moon's surface, and is 2 miles wide. It appears to be an engineered creation which means it could be about what on Earth we call an man-made creation, ergo created by Someone!

Elsewhere, Dr. Wilkins stated:

Two questions come to life: how come this structure has existed for such a long time? Why was it only seen today and not subjected to external influences - such as meteorite impacts? How did it happen that this bridge was built so quickly? And since it is an engineered creation, a whole field of speculation opens up. Anyway - this is the most interesting creation whether artificial or natural that has been discovered with a telescope.

The existence of a formation called "Lunar Bridge" or "O'Neill's Bridge"[136] has not been explained satisfactorily to this day. Attempts have been made to explain it by optical illusion - as suggested by the likes of H. Oberdonfer, P. Příhoda, A. Ruckl, J. Sadil. Their other colleagues were more specific, and the existence of the bridge was also confirmed by Soviet scientist Gavrilov. On the other hand, the Italian researcher Antonini stated that: The existence of this bridge seems likely... Today this bridge is no longer there - in its place are two small craters...

Pons O'Neilli existed and could really be found between two rocky capes: Promonthium Olivium to the north and Promonthium Lavinium to the south, about 10 km north of Yerkes crater on the western shore of the Solstice Sea - at E 51° and N 16°. Today there are indeed two craters there. Would this be a coincidence and a game of chance? Or perhaps we really witnessed some construction work testifying to the existence and activity of an alien Mind on our closest neighbor in Space, and 16 years before our astronauts???...

The bridge on the Moon was not the only such phenomenon observed there, as less than a year after the O'Neill Bridge - on May 16, 1954 - Prof. Frazer Thompson of Tulane University (USA) reported the discovery of a completely new fissure in Piccolomini Crater - at S 29°.7 and E 32°.2 - from which leads a

---

[136] The astronomy literature also wrote about the "Bridge of Achilles" - *Pons Achillesi*.

straight lane 300 meters wide and resembling a highway or runway!..

In March 1955, the indefatigable Dr. Wilkins reported the observation in the Solstice Sea of a resulting pit with vertical walls!

A puzzling new formation was discovered in 1985 by Felix A. Bach in the vicinity of Rost crater - at S 56°.4 and W 33°.7. This object was in the shape of a pillar with 7 onion-shaped formations attached to it. The height of this "pillar" must have been at least 20 miles, or about 36 km!!!

A year later, Felix Bach observed the same pillar, but it was located above Schiller crater - at S 51°,8 and W 40°,0 - also this mystery was not solved...

All this I read from old astronomy textbooks and in the selenological literature until the late 1970s. The strange thing - nowadays there is no mention of this in the literature! Draw your own conclusions from this, Reader. Someone cares a lot that all these facts should be forgotten as soon as possible...

Košice, November 27, 1999

***

I had already translated this paper in January 2000, hence all this could already be written in the context of the past - the 20th century.

If Dr. Jesenský had written what was announced by "The Mars Mission" group led by Dr. Richard Hoagland - the picture would have been even more complete. After all, TMM has shown that something is happening on the Moon and Mars all the time, and by no means on our initiative!...

"And what has all this to do with TM?" the Reader will rightly ask - and it will be right. And it has - and a lot! I think that the study of the Moon and other planets will be helpful in solving this mystery, because it came to us from the Cosmos, and there we should look for its solution. And only there. There is no question - we must return to the Silver Globe. Intuition tells me that there lies the key to this mystery, as well as to the mystery of UFOs and many, many others. And this is already a task for us - people of the 21st century and the Third Millennium.

We have to go back to the moon. I don't know when we'll do it, but it's a necessity, because it's our natural base for systemic and out-of-system flights, as well as a place for possible Contact with Aliens (if they exist and operate in the Solar System), because I think they're waiting for us there!

And in 2025...

***

And now let me, Reader, introduce you to the opinions of some Polish unorthodox astronomers and ufologists who have something to say about TM. The first of these is an astronomer from Giżycko - mentioned already here several times, M.Sc. Roman Rzepka, whose theory is an incredibly interesting variant of the E2-65 hypothesis from CANON, and for this reason I propose to adopt for it the designation E2-65a.

11. R. Rzepka - HYPOTHESIS #86: ORGANIC METEORITE?

You never know what could happen... - I remembered the Polish adage, reading a letter from Robert Leśniakiewicz - a man of extraordinary passion, an undisputed expert in many fields of knowledge from the so-called "borderlands". And it was written to me by the hand of Mr. Robert that I had to "do" an essay entitled "What was the Tunguska meteorite?".

For God's sake (!), if I had known with certainty what this unusual event was, and had announced it long ago, I would have saved many hundreds, perhaps thousands of hectares of forest converted into paper, onto which many hundreds of "certain" theories were poured. What's more, Mr. Robert fixate my name in the projected book as the voice of a specialist-meteorologist. I am not formally a specialist in this field, but I know a little about chemistry and for years I have been exploring for entertainment the mysteries of stones falling from the sky, with undisguised trepidation I decided to describe my thoughts on the great mystery of the Tunguska phenomenon.

As if to justify my decision, I was reminded of a well-known saying by Georges Clemenceau: "War is too serious a thing to be entrusted to generals." Not being a "general," I can say with full responsibility that I grasp the "generalist" specialized viewpoints on the matter. The unraveling of the TM mystery seems to be hampered by a rigid approach to the principles of cosmic mechanics, ruling out the possibility of intergalactic exchange of matter. I can afford to take a different view on the matter. By the way, the nature of TP is better conveyed by the term used in the English-language literaturę as *Tunguska blast*[137], because it more accurately reflects the current state of knowledge on the subject.

The event in the bend of the Podkamennaya Tunguska River cannot be treated as a unique rarity in isolation from other - sometimes seemingly distant - events, phenomena or finds. It is worth recalling at this point the observation of a spectacular event in the village of Roboziero[138] near Moscow. There, in the monastery of St. Kirill (Cyril), the records of the interrogation of witnesses, eyewitnesses of the phenomenon involving the falling from a cloudless sky straight onto the surface of Lake Roboziero of burning embers of some matter, have been preserved to modern times. When the research of the eminent scientist Chladni confirmed the reality of meteorites in the early 19th century, attempts were made to explain the Roboziero mystery as a meteorite fall. However, this was considered a false clue, since the burning matter on the lake, if it were a meteorite, once extinguished it would not have ignited repeatedly and on the surface of the water, burning for a total of one and a half hours. And the just precisely documented phenomenon proves conclusively one thing! - the remains of an organic meteorite fell on the surface of Robozier, and this is exactly how the whole

---

[137] Tunguska explosion.
[138] On August 15, 1663.

phenomenon should look like, as described in the chronicles of St. Cyril's Monastery.

I used the term organic meteorite, which science does not know because... such meteorites do not exist. But for sure?

The Roboziero phenomenon is quite easily explained by this type of matter. A mixture of many organic compounds - about which more later - inherently has a specific gravity less than that of water, so it must float on top of it. The frozen and solidified mass of such a meteorite gradually released its liquid and volatile components, which fed more and more into the flammable mixture and smoldered its mineral components - such as iron sulfides - which could in all likelihood have been there. Rusty-brown stains on the water could only be evidence of sulfide oxidation.

Another phenomenon could have occurred there as well. The mineral-laden lump of organic meteorite could have plunged into the lake's depths, releasing its gaseous fractions in the water, which, obviously flowing in gaseous bubbles to the surface, fed the substance burning on the surface.

On January 14, 1993, at 18:50 in Jerzmanowice near Kraków, a "bolt from the blue" mercilessly exposed the doctrinaire approach to such phenomena. And it was also an organic meteorite of the kind that... "nonexistent". Different times, different civilization enclave. Here, the meteorite revealed another of its characteristics, which previously - in the case of Robozier - it could not reveal. Exploding in Jerzmanowice, it scattered colloidal particles of carbon (soot, graphite) over the local area, which, like graphite bombs dropped on Belgrade during the last Balkan war, ravaged the surrounding electric power infrastructure with known consequences.

Years ago, I once accidentally found an unusual stone in the area. Its unremarkable appearance and my intuition told me of its unearthly origin. But that's a different story. However, this episode has since made these "unearthly treasures" an incurable hobby of mine.

In my free time - which seems to be getting less and less - I wander around the Mazurian wilderness looking for unusual cosmic visitors.

I managed to find several specimens of strange matter, so strange that basically no one knows what it is!!! So the obvious course of action was that I sent (and stubbornly knowing my own - I still do) samples of the find to people who should quickly identify them. I assure you that this mostly involved the biggest names in the field of extraterrestrial matter research. I generally met with a lot of kindness from these people, for which I am very grateful.

However, it turned out that the same sample, depending on the the continent where it was studied was: post-industrial waste, fresh volcanic tuff, some undefined product of soil-forming processes... It could also be a meteorite, but... is not - I have such "expertise" also! And all because the metallic iron particles found in the strange matter do not contain nickel. The particles of iron found at the site of the Tunguska explosion also do not contain nickel. It should be mentioned here that Apollo 11-17 missions brought back samples of lunar regolith, in which tiny shreds of metallic iron also do not contain nickel. The absence of this element disqualifies the samples as to further detailed studies, such as the isotopic composition of oxygen in its compounds, as in silicates or oxides. This would essentially be a conclusive study, since the proportions of its three isotopes: $16O : 17O : 18O$ are as unique in every part of the Cosmos as fingerprint lines are in every person.

Necessarily, organic matter that can be sensed organoleptically - by smell - has never been examined in a sample. And this matter resembles very much the matter described in the literature as it should be in interstellar space! This mainly concerns a mixture of polycyclic aromatic hydrocarbons, referred to by the commonly accepted English acronym PAHs.

A well-known feature of this type of chemical compounds is their explosive combustion (oxidation) under certain conditions, especially in a highly fragmented state into an air-colloidal suspension.[139] At this point it is worth mentioning the remarkable people of NASA Ames Research Center and their achievements to date. Namely, they have found that interstellar space contains untold amounts of organic compounds that are the result of complex photochemical processes occurring there. The particles of interstellar dust, these amiable perhaps a little unconventionally working gentlemen Max Bernstein and Lou Allamondola, obtain from the upper layers of the Earth's atmosphere with the help of the legendary U-2 airplane, or by dabbling on roofs (literally!) they pull it from rain gutters.

---

[139] A similar principle drives the operation of the thermobaric bomb, which is a weapon with a strike force comparable to a small-caliber nuclear weapon.

So it turns out that interstellar dust containing a number of organic compounds reaches Earth!

The aforementioned team put forward a pioneering theory that the origin of some meteorites is comets visiting our solar system. This is absolute heresy! - because until now it was believed that all meteorites - with the exception of Martian and lunar ones - came from the Planetoid Belt, and the carbonaceous ones from the outer part of it - the one closer to Jupiter.

I am convinced that soon this dogma too - also thanks to the research of the aforementioned scientists - will be debunked, it will be proven that the carbonaceous meteorites, and especially their organic fraction, come from outside the Solar System. The carbonaceous meteorites Murchinson (Australia), which fell to Earth in September 1969, and the Tagish Lake (Canada) carbonaceous meteorite, which landed in the lake of that name on January 18, 2000, proved to be extremely interesting.

It turned out that these meteorites contain a wide variety of compounds that, when sprayed into the air, can create extremely powerful explosive mixtures.[140] These meteorites contain a few to several percent of organic matter mixed with the mineral fraction. Thus, it is easy to see that it is possible to have organic matter content that exceeds significantly 50% of the object's mass. It would be difficult to call them anything other than organic meteors. In the existing classification of "unearthly stones" such a

---

[140] Some comet researchers claim that their heads contain a very powerful explosive - azobenzol - $N_2C_{12}H_{10}$, which may explain their explosive decay or splitting of comet nuclei.

term does not appear, because simply such stones have not been identified so far.

Not identified, because it is a priori assumed that objects of this type, even if they existed in space, would, by virtue of their fragility[141] have no chance to tear through the Earth's atmosphere. The prevailing view is that only stone or iron meteorites are able to tear through the atmosphere and land on the Earth's surface. This forgets a very important issue - the heat conduction coefficient. An iron meteorite flying through the atmosphere as a result of friction with the air quickly heats up its surface, melts and burns with much greater intensity than a poorly heat-conducting rock, and in addition, non-flammable.

A lump of deeply frozen mixtures of liquid organic compounds may behave even differently in its fall. One of the most famous organic meteorites - Orgueil - is so fragile and delicate that many researchers wonder how it could have survived its murderous flight through our atmosphere. Well, it could, because today it is porous, but when it left the cold emptiness of the Cosmos, there were liquid and volatile frozen components in its present pores that made it not at all brittle and delicate, but quite the opposite!

As for the fact that the perpetrator of the Tunguska explosion was a Cosmic Visitor, there is general agreement. In fact, it is difficult to have a different opinion on this subject. However, what the nature of this newcomer was, what it was, is another matter entirely, here the range of proposals is very wide: from the crash

---

[141] And most importantly the chemical composition...

of a manned UFO spacecraft, a black hole, a ball of antimatter to an asteroid and a comet.

Science eventually accepted as the prevailing version, the theory formulated by three American researchers, C.F. Chyba, P.J. Thomas and K.J. Zahni. It may come as a surprise, however, that the theory of the gentlemen mentioned here generally disregards the obvious, undeniable facts of the Tunguska Big Bang, and even contradicts them in many places. Namely, they assumed that the cause of the Tunguska explosion was the intrusion into Earth's atmosphere of a massive asteroid originating from the asteroid belt between Mars and Jupiter. Leaving aside many details of this theory, it is worth noting that the asteroid in question would have had a diameter of 60 m and entered the atmosphere at a speed of about 15 km/s. Such parameters were chosen because they were needed to get the needed energy of the shock wave!...

According to them, the asteroid exploded due to the pressure gradient created in the object. Chyba's proposed stony asteroid sought to flatten into something like a "pie"[142], as a result, it changed shape(!) this expansion increased atmospheric drag to the point that the object disintegrated explosively.

Outlined in summary, the gist of this theory was announced by C.F. Chyba in the pages of the prestigious Nature. Chyba's theory was applauded - de facto proclaiming it as an incontrovertible fact - by professional journals, including "Sky & Telescope" No. 3/1993 - with an article on the subject titled

---

[142] What about the plasticity of solid rock???... - footnote R. Rzepka.

"Tunguska: An Asteroid"[143]. And on this modern science has the proverbial dot the i's and cross the t's.

Thus, the hitherto prevailing theory taking into account the intrusion of some part of the comet into the Earth's atmosphere was rejected. Any contestation in such cases, and especially from non-professionals, is a profanation of the great names and the fruits of their intellectual efforts - *Roma faculta, causa finita!*

And I, a brazen profaner - and an "exoprofaner, after my favorite Asimov - holed up in the silence of a Masurian town, late at night writing these words - dare to disagree with Mr. C. F. Chyba and his team! They are simply wrong! One thing I can agree with is that the perpetrator of the great Tunguska explosion was a space alien.

A little about the history of the Tunguska object research. The first to try to pry the great mystery from Nature in 1908 was Leonid Kulik. This modest young employee of the Museum of Mineralogy in Moscow seems to have been the first man who, overcoming a thorny (literally and figuratively) road, embraced with his eyes from the top of Mount Shacherma an image unimaginable by its scale of the enormity of the destruction.

Kulik's first expedition, due to his unfamiliarity with the conditions and terrain, was short but fruitful. It clarified the cartographic data of the area, described the visible effects of the destruction of the stand of trees, the characteristic features of the destruction, but the most important, Kulik stated, was the absence of an impact crater. After such a gigantic explosion, it was

---

[143] "The Tunguska bolide is an asteroid".

inconceivable that it was not there! Some sources say that Kulik, searching there for the expected lumps of cosmic iron in huge quantities, which he obviously did not find - neither he nor anyone after him - found extremely fine shreds of metallic iron with the help of a magnet. Later laboratory tests rejected their connection to the big bang! As it happens, the most active group in studying this phenomenon are Russians (hardly surprising, by the way). Some scholars from the Universities of Tomsk and Moscow have devoted their entire creative lives in an attempt to answer the question: Что это было?

Dr. A. P. Bojarkina from Tomsk took part in more than 35 expeditions to the Podkamennaya Tunguska, which made her stay there longer than in her studio at the University. Science owes a lot to her expeditions, and when it comes to acquiring research material in the form of samples of vegetation, soil, etc. - she seems to have no equal. Nevertheless, her great enthusiasm and effort have not resulted in spectacular discoveries. At least, this is the impression one gets from studying the literature on the subject.

The orthodox approach of many scientists with post-impact craters encoded in their heads, tons of space rocks and iron lumps containing > 5% nickel and a few other truths, but referring in the end to a small section of the vastness of the diversity of cosmic matter seem to have missed the evidence pointing to the true nature of the cosmic visitor.

It even seems that some facts seem to be inconveniently, discreetly bypassed.

Well, because what to do when there is not what "should be", and there is what "should not be"! A detailed study of the soil revealed an unnaturally high concentration of a number of rare elements in it.

This "unnaturally" high content of them is, of course, the scale of ppm[144] - or μg/g. a very characteristic feature of their occurrence is that the areas of concentration form many separate points. This may prove one thing, that the elements reached the Earth during many simultaneously exploding, but separate "charges". I mentioned a perplexing fact - the elements do not match in mutual quantitative proportions any of the known cosmic objects. They don't match, because they can't match!...

In the deposits of peat there, a perplexing detail was discovered in a layer dated 1908 - namely, soot, or amorphous carbon. So far, no natural phenomenon of this type is known, in which such a thing is formed. Well, after all, where would soot come from, if the explosion is caused solely by a pressure gradient between the front part of a lump of iron or rock and its back part? However, it is known that such a form of amorphous carbon is formed during the combustion of, for example, hydrocarbons - this includes the combustion of PAHs - under oxygen-deficient conditions.

Under optimal conditions, the aforementioned compounds burn to CO_2 and H_2O. The soot was found because it simply should have been there!...

I mentioned that particularly perplexing and consistently silent in the literature is the fact of finding at the site of the explosion particles of pure metallic iron and millimeter-sized globules that are almost pure fused (amorphous) silica (SiO_2) with

---

[144] Parts per million.

small admixtures of metal silicates, but only up to and including iron.

These strange things were found there because they should be there!!! I write this paragraph in a somewhat ironic tone. To those offended by this, I apologize, but somehow otherwise I find it difficult to articulate without emotion my opinion on the subject.

The scenario of the event on the morning of June 30, 1908 over the Siberian taiga probably looked like this:

Toward Earth, against the wishes and prohibitions of astronomers, an organic meteoroid of considerable size flies from the interstellar abyss.

It is made up mainly of the building blocks there, so for the most part it consists of high-energy carbon and hydrogen compounds. "Spiced" with a small amount of silicate dust and particles of pure iron from a super giant exploding somewhere, in which the process of nuclear fusion proceeds in such a way that the final product is various types of heavy elements such as carbon, magnesium, silicon, sulfur and iron. Supergiants reach the end of their lives - they explode when a large amount of iron is deposited in their nuclei. A further series of elements is formed as a result of a peculiar cosmic transformation of matter, in which the products of the supergiant are the starting ingredients of new accretion processes.

"Luckily" the flight of the exotic galactic visitor follows the tangent to the Earth's orbit, and the meteoroid's direction of flight is consistent with the orbital motion of our planet. It catches up with the Earth, which flashes along its orbit at a speed of about 30 km/s. There is a relative reduction in the speed of the meteoroid in relation to the Earth - so much so that the Earth's gravity intercepts the galactic visitor and directs it towards its surface. The meteoroid, breaking through the thickening layers of the atmosphere, loses much of its mass and speed. At this point astronomers say that an object with a low specific gravity, fragile and delicate does not a chance to get through the atmosphere. So what? - aware of its misery, frightened, should turn back! - and what does Mr. Newton say about it?

However, at this point, so fragile and fragile, he was not! It was a hard, deep-frozen mixture of the ingredients I mentioned earlier, and on top of that it had low thermal conductivity. The pressure gradient generated in the object reached a critical magnitude, tearing the entire object to pieces - and this is the beginning of a long, vaporous explosion. Individual fragments of the parent body, battered by the huge turbulence undergo further dispersion.

Finally, a gigantic dust-air cloud flashes toward Earth. Mixed with air, it ignites and explodes over the Siberian taiga. Molten solidified silicate droplets, mineral interstellar dust, iron metallic shreds fall to the ground in this infernal heat. All this mixes with the water produced in huge quantities during the explosion and forms a dirty, muddy rain.

In this muddy rain, soot - pure amorphous carbon - also falls to the ground as a result of the inaccurate combustion of some of the organic substances - mainly hydrocarbons.

The rapidity of the meteorite's dispersion did not allow its dust and aerosols to mix thoroughly with the air, and, moreover, there was simply too little oxygen in the entire space covered by the object's disintegration to balance the reaction - i.e. to burn the carbon completely.

A brief analysis of the results of the Podkamiennaya Tunguska site, presented here, allows us to formulate the thesis that the cause of the gigantic explosion of June 30, 1908 was the intrusion into the Earth's atmosphere of a gigantic meteoroid, several tens of meters in diameter, similar in composition to the Orgueil Meteorite, but with a much higher content - reaching 80-90% - of organic substances, mainly carbon and hydrogen compounds.

The now-forgotten case of the mysterious explosion in Jerzmanowice near Krakow seems to be similarly "unexplained" as TM. After all, these are twin - aside from the scale - cases! If science had gone to even a little trouble, there probably would have been a chance to find carbon particles on the insulators of power lines responsible for the characteristic damage to electrical installations and equipment in the area of the mysterious phenomenon. Or maybe it's worth digging into the gutters as well...

Circulating in orbits that collide with the Earth, thousands of larger or smaller asteroids are a real threat to our planet, but not fatal!

The end of all this will be put by an interstellar, uninvited - or perhaps delegated! - visitor, eager for our terrestrial oxygen. It seems that TM is just a small reconnoiterer for a future visit.

Giżycko, 24.06.2001.

***

Brrr... - reading the last paragraph of Mr. Roman Rzepka's article, a person gets stuffy and cold. Would it be true? Let's look at it coolly and without emotion. Hasn't something like this already happened? Some hydrocarbon-frozen-to-the-bone space projectile hit Mars, converting oxygen from its atmosphere into carbon dioxide, and due to the greenhouse effect, this caused its annealing and evaporation of water from its oceans. The continents stood in their motion, and giant shield volcanoes began to form over the "hot spots" - Olympus Mons (Nix Olympica), Arsia Mons, Ascraeus Mons, Pavonis Mons or Elysium Mons... - whose emissions only exacerbated the greenhouse effect. This impact could have happened about 100,000 years ago - at the end of the Tertiary. The same could have happened to Venus as well...

And now, from a different angle. The starting point of the excellent novel by Krzysztof Boruń and Andrzej Trepka titled "Proxima" is the discovery of a carbonaceous meteorite, which consisted of pure anthracite. It came from the Proxima planetary system and was the remains of a planet that was destroyed by the inhabitants of this system during its reconstruction. Who knows if the two Authors didn't hit the bull's eye and the writing intuition didn't deviate from reality???... Maybe TM really was just not enough of a newcomer from another planetary system, and it was inadvertently sent into Space by our Brothers in Sense???...

On July 17, 2001, I received a letter from Kazimierz Bzowski, a well-known Warsaw ufologist, who gives in it some interesting facts having to do with TM. Let me, Reader, present it with slight abbreviations, because it is worth it...

12. K. Bzowski - COSMOLOTE OR... GREAT DRAGON?

In the summer of 1980, Wanda Konarzewska's program on the Polish Public Television's second program titled. "Mail to the Alpha Club" addressed the TM mystery. At the time, the presenter asked viewers to ask anyone with their own opinion on the subject to write it down and send it to Polish Television. I then scribbled down an 8-page A-4 format elaboration and sent it in. To my astonishment, after two months it turned out that the six most interesting statements were selected, and among them mine and the authors were invited to the studio for another program about the incident, and here is my view in a nutshell:

The nuclear-powered spacecraft entered Earth's atmosphere with the intention of landing, but its sensors detected that the area intended for landing (the taiga) was actually a compacted mass of living matter. The ship's automatic safeguards - forbidding the destruction of life - acted and the ship, from its flight descending toward Earth, attempted to break out of the updraft. Then the jet of recoil hit the taiga, causing trees to be knocked down over a large area and in an elongated, rolling path.

The sudden huge overload caused the equipment to malfunction and, as a result, the nuclear reactor exploded. Therefore, no remains of the facility were found on Earth, while the trees standing vertically at the epicenter of the explosion confirm this version of events. The long-lasting irradiation of the area with gamma rays also confirms that.

In general - my current view of the matter has not changed much, except that what exploded was not the "main object" that entered the Solar System, but a reconnaissance ship to identify landing conditions, the reaction of the [Earth's] inhabitants, etc. Only it malfunctioned and exploded due to a nuclear reaction. A similar opinion is also held by Eng. Miłosław Wilk, whose drawing of the lander I included in my book titled "Sieć Wilka" on p. 133. according to him, it was an automatic, unmanned reconnaissance.

In the fall of 1980, TVP-2 held a meeting in front of the camera of these invitees. Among them was Mr. Jozef Skarzynski from Zduńska Wola, who was then in his 80s, and who, as an 8-year-old boy, had been in exile with his father (after the 1905 revolution) in a village 760 kilometers from Podkamennaya Tunguska, and was just going to school at the time of the incident... He came to the program with his two granddaughters, who took care of him. So far, this is the only living witness to the incident that I was able to meet. Schools there before the Bolshevik Revolution were open in spring and summer (excluding summer vacations), as only during these periods could one get to them on foot. Little Józio had about 2 km to school. Below is his account, which I noted down during the program:

As I walked toward the school, it suddenly became so quiet that neither birdsong nor the rustle of the wind could be heard... Despite my will, I walked slower and slower, listening to this silence... The whole world around me turned yellow. Everything turned yellow... the sky, my hands, the trees and the leaves on them... In horror, I stood and watched, not understanding what was happening. I don't know how long it lasted... but I saw the color of the surroundings change to orange... At that moment I turned around and ran towards my house. There was my father and several neighbors, the same deportees. My father had all the windows and even the mirrors covered, candles were lit...

My father told me not to go anywhere and to pray with them, because they thought the end of the world was approaching, but who would keep watch over me! I was tempted to see what was going on outside. Through a crack in the shawl covering the window, I saw the whole environment gradually change color - through red to dark beetroot, brown and black. Although everything was black, it was not dark. A silvery light was coming from somewhere. They didn't uphold me, I got outside... and I saw: on the horizon from the ground, all the way up into the sky you could see a kind of "waterfall" pouring from above - as if of glowing molten metal... - but everything around was black. All this lasted until late afternoon, about eight hours.

***

Please forgive me a digression, Reader. Such darkness in the middle of the day is mentioned by many people - including my grandfather - who experienced the TP. Isn't this reminiscent of the description of the raid on Earth by the mysterious Black Cloud from Fred Hoyle's novel "The Black Cloud"? In that case, it would appear that TM was accompanied by a dense cloud of cosmic matter, which was also pulled by the power of our planet's gravity into the atmosphere and partially burned up in it... This story gives food for thought, because then we would have to assume that there are meteorite swarms and clouds of cosmic "dust" traveling at hyperbolic speeds, perhaps even of organic origin, which from time to time haunt the Solar System and can cause the phenomenon of Great Extinctions or Ice Ages???...

But let's go back to Kazimierz Bzowski's letter:

***

Case number two: establishing the date of the event through interrogation of the local Tungusic peoples (Evenks) by Leonid Kulik's expedition in 1927 and later. In my opinion, they could not remember "the event of June 30, 1908" for the simple reason that they did not know such concepts as: "calendar," "month of June," and "date." They could and certainly did remember other events in the sky, which they could remember, but which, in turn, Kulik did not need to know about. Why? Primarily - astronomy at that time did not know as much as it does today, and secondly - because there were no computers then.

I give the data obtained from an astronomical computer program, and which relate to solar eclipses in a similar period, with the parameters for making observations I entered as "Podkamennaya Tunguska", approximate location - N 65° and E 095° because I do not know the exact one. Level 200 m above sea level. Time according to GMT - hence it may seem strange sunrise in the afternoon...[145]

---

[145] The local time of Podkamennaya Tunguska is Irkutsk time - IRKT or

The blue color distinguishes the solar eclipse that the Tungusic peoples may have remembered. For them, the event looked as if the Great Dragon had eaten the Sun, hence the dating is slightly different from that of European or American observers.

Thus, it was either a cosmolote or a... Great Dragon!

Warsaw, July 12, 2001

***

Hm... - the concept of the cosmolote as issued by Kazimir Bzowski, is a variant of the A-14 hypothesis from Privalov's CANON OF HIPOTES OF THE TM. The interesting thing about it is that the alien lander broke down and exploded. Or maybe the aliens wanted to land on the Gobi, but miscalculated and their lander simply crashed several hundred kilometers further north than they intended?...

The Tungusic peoples, like the tribes of Africa or the Australian Aborigines, do not know the concept of time as we understand it. Nevertheless, I can't imagine that they could make a cluster of two events: a solar eclipse and a TM fall into one TP. No, such a thing is highly unlikely. Besides, after all, both phenomena were observed by educated Russians, Poles, Chinese and other people residing in these areas, over a considerable territory of Russia and Mongolia and China. And they did so independently of each other. Thus, this hypothesis, ranked in the group of D hypotheses in CANON... does not seem to be

GMT + 7h.

accurate, although it would be a mistake not to consider it in our deliberations.

And now another author and another point of view...

13. M. Mioduszewski - TUNGUSKA METEORITE: A BIG EXPLOSION AND A BIG PROBLEM

„It is nothing that things happen.

But it is everything that we find out about them"

Egon Friedell

When I was offered the opportunity to express my opinion in this work, I was very happy to have the honor of speaking alongside such distinguished researchers and scientists. On the other hand, I acquired some concerns. These were related to the fact that this topic is extremely complex and intricate. So, while preparing to write these words, I decided to once again review the materials available to me on the subject of the Tunguska Explosion, as well as to study in depth the finished part of the script of the "Siberian Bolide" itself, which was made available to me.

I firmly resolved to myself that this time I would finally, at all costs, try to address this incident unequivocally and advocate one of the hypotheses. After just a few hours of digging through various materials, I quickly realized that such a notion was naive, to say the least. On the contrary, the more thoroughly I learned about the results of the research and analysis, the more confusion arose in my mind. Finally, I concluded that not only would I not come to a clear view, but I was increasingly distant from any opinion on the event that shook Siberia on June 30, 1908.

By way of explanation, I would like to mention that as a member of the former Lesser Poland Research Center for UFOs and Anomalous Phenomena, I have always been interested in this event, but this interest was quite specific. This is because I treated it as another in a series of many mysteries of history, which must be accepted as fact, and with which it is virtually unknown what to do next. It may seem to readers that this was a manifestation of my ignorance of the subject, but this is untrue. After all, it is one thing to actively deal with mysteries that are not only "younger", but also literally, "geographically" closer, and another to be interested in a matter so distant, the details of which we can only learn from various book publications or articles. In addition, in recent years few new facts have appeared in the Tunguska Meteorite issue (although, looking at the totality of similar events in the world, we got a powerful research and, above all, comparative material!). However, the proposal to write a chapter for a book about the mysterious eruption over Siberia interested me a lot, as it became a chance for me to look at the event in more detail.

Of course, I will not hide, I am not an expert on the subject, nor do I consider myself competent to give a conclusive and unequivocal opinion. I also do not want to duplicate the facts and data contained in other parts of this work, but I will nevertheless try to look at the matter through the eyes of a person involved in the study of the phenomenon of Unidentified Flying Objects and make some of my comments and observations.

First of all, after just reviewing the materials for publication in this book, I became convinced that the Siberian Bolide, or if you prefer the Tunguska Meteorite, is one big bag into which literally everything - almost every possible hypothesis to explain this event - has been thrown. As the reader himself had the opportunity to see, there are more than 100 such "explanations", more or less serious! I think that at this point no one is surprised anymore that it is difficult to form an opinion on this subject. So I decided not to add any more theories to it, because they will certainly not bring anything new to the matter, except possibly confusion.

The indisputable fact remains that something happened in the Podkamennaya Tunguska area, which, although it left a material trace, still deftly eludes by all possible means any explanation. And it's no wonder that the research and expeditions conducted for more than 90 years still have not yielded satisfactory results. For how could they, anyway? What researchers have at their disposal is only the traces that the "Tunguska Unusual Thing" left behind, a handful of accounts from people who may have seen the flight of this "something" through the skies of Siberia, some accounts of strange events in the world at the time, and a vast, immense number of extreme hypotheses. It's not easy to move smoothly in this, let alone investigate!

One thing we know for sure - on the morning of the last day of June 1908, something happened in Siberia that looked like the fall of a meteorite or other cosmic body... Only to a certain extent, because it turned out that a) it lacked a post-impact crater, b) the object performed maneuvers before the explosion, c) it did not leave behind a single ounce (at least found!) of the matter it carried with it, and so on and so forth... It seems to me that it is worthwhile in all this to distinguish three main currents of theories explaining this event:

1. Cosmic body that entered the Earth's atmosphere - in this group I would include all meteors, bolides, plasmids and other "natural" cosmic creations.

2. Terrestrial phenomenon associated with various phenomena such as a gas explosion.

3. Various forms of interference of alien CNTs in the Earth's atmosphere, whether intentional or accidental.

In addition, another point comes to mind, which is a combination of the previous three:

4. Accidental overlap of several of the above-mentioned factors.

A whole host of theories, their modifications and mutations have been cultivated on the basis of just these four groups. I realize that the above four points are a far-reaching simplification, but at the same time this is the only idea I can think of in terms of sorting out what perhaps needs to be proven about the Tunguska Meteorite. And there is much to prove, for the plethora of contradictory facts creates quite a bit of confusion in this story. Contradictory facts, but only apparently... I suppose they all fit perfectly into one whole, perhaps the issue is in the proper view of the case and the course of events, or maybe there is still some missing piece of this puzzle that has not been found?

And now let me move on to more specific considerations regarding the mysterious event in the Siberian sky. May Readers forgive me for omitting here the most, in my opinion, plausible explanations, namely the hypothesis of a cosmic body that fell into the Earth's atmosphere and exploded, and Earth's natural phenomena. I do this consciously, and my explanation is that, firstly, many excellent scientists have already commented on them, and secondly, I myself am not an expert in this field, so out of respect for the Reader and the matter itself, I will not dwell on it. However, I would like, as a person associated with the study of UFOs, to discuss the topic of hypothesis No. 2. In order to move unproblematically in this area, one must, willingly or unwillingly, adopt that part of ufological knowledge, which is already indisputably alienology - that is, knowledge of hypothetical alien CNTs. Not counting the dubious quality of revelations á la Roswell, the beautiful but how naive fairy tales of the likes of Bob Lazar or John Lear, this knowledge is relatively modest and uncertain. This is a fact. But there is a vast amount of data in it, which, while we can't interpret clearly, we can plug into sundry events. And that's what we're going to do.

The first thing to realize at this point of consideration is that the "extraterrestrial theory" is remarkably convenient, because it allows us to explain almost everything without difficulty. And the fact that it is convenient means that it is all too easy to succumb to it, or worse, to be convinced of its 100% truthfulness, closing oneself off to other explanations. So, exercising all caution, let's delve into a few details that don't make me feel comfortable.

My first observation is that it is actually very deft to connect the theory of a vehicle (manned or unmanned) of an alien CNT with a "natural" space body. How? It's simple. First of all, assume that the CNT in question, since it has reached us, is ahead of us in development perhaps by some 10,000 years or even more. Since, therefore, it has sufficiently advanced technology to cover such distances in one way or another, it must be a highly reliable technology. Thus, it should not be difficult for such a CNT to build a vehicle that operates effectively in the Earth's atmosphere. Thus, one can further assume that its failure rate would be extremely low, perhaps even close to zero. However, something could always happen that would result in the vehicle not being able to return to its mothership, nay - it would simply fall to the planet's surface. And then what? The answer can be found even in our time. The mechanism would be the same as for modern spy planes - self-destruction of all or part of key equipment and apparatus. And what's the best way to ensure that no one suspects any outside interference? A flyby and explosion of, for example, a meteorite should be simulated! Wouldn't that even be a perfect way to mask a failed mission?

If such a scenario actually took place, we would not be able to prove much. I would like to show, using this hypothesis as an example, that if someone wants to prove variant two of the TM explanation, he starts the proverbial tilting at windmills. The only thing that would save this path to explaining the event would be to find debris that undeniably comes from outside the Earth and is an artificial creation! And this, as we know, has not been found, at least no one has proven it. What does this prove? Well, that it is naive to think that an alien CNT would leave its vehicle for dead, along with its remains, thus giving proof of its existence. This is a preposterous claim that calls into question the fact that this CNT is really intelligent. Of course, all of this loses its meaning if we assume that the TM was in fact the lander of a spaceplane or even the cosmolote itself, which had just arrived somewhere from a distant planetary system and, during maneuvers in orbit or in the atmosphere, malfunctioned - in which case, perhaps, there would be no one left to rescue its crew, as they would have been the ones who crashed.

Again, you can see how fluid are the boundaries of the theories that fit under the common term of alien CNT vehicle or terrestrial ancient civilization[146]. Therefore, it is worth realizing that unequivocally proving outright the fact that the Siberian bolide was some kind of space vehicle of another civilization is impossible. So how else can it be done? Only by elimination - if you show what TM could not be, it will be easier to argue hypotheses of the type of explanation No. 2. In my opinion, this is the only right way. It does not deny the interference of artificial flying apparatuses in the event, and at the same time it does not exclude, and even stimulates the investigation of theories about the cosmic body or terrestrial natural phenomena.

I would like to point out that the natural explanations, that is, No. 1 and No. 3, are still the most close to me. Too many facts clearly point to them, especially if some kind of meteorite or comet is involved. And here there is still a free field for scientists, whose task is to explain the whole puzzling phenomena. After all, no one said that everything is already known about the falls of these bodies into the Earth's atmosphere; on the contrary, this is only the beginning of this study.

Meanwhile, let's return to these 100 hypotheses. There is everything there! The only thing missing is Godzilla (because Yeti

---

[146] I agree with the views proclaimed, among others, by R. Leśniakiewicz and Dr. M. Jesensky about the "War of the Gods" of 10,000 - 12,000 years ago and the remnants of it, which we have the misfortune to encounter.

is already recurring!) along with the Terminator! Looking at the Tunguska Meteorite from the side, one can see that not only, the event is a press evergreen as Robert Leśniakiewicz wrote in the introduction to this work, but also a universal explanation of almost everything unexplained so far. Too many people try to allege TM as proof of this or that. I'm just waiting to hear that it was actually a fragment of Atlantis that fell after our ancestors were taken into space with all the land by aliens... Alternatively, it could be some other load of nonsense. And in fact, it is evidence of only one thing, that on June 30, 1908, some body flew over the Podkamennaya Tunguska region after which it exploded with the force of at least 10 Mt TNT, causing a whole mixture of accompanying phenomena. What was it? To date, no one knows for sure. It is very easy to encase this incident in further improbable hypotheses and prove them at all costs, even if they not match. But is that the point? Certainly not!

And yet, despite its mysteriousness, the Siberian bolide and all the facts related to it, point us to something very important. Such a huge event, an obvious powerful explosion, has all the time eluded all attempts at a clear explanation. The most powerful minds are puzzling over this problem, trying to solve it at all costs - without result. A great explosion and a great problem, unsolvable even for the science of the early 21st century. Whatever was the cause of this event, we were, we are and who knows how long we will be vulnerable to such "visitors". This should give us all a lot to think about.

Kraków, July 20, 2001

***

Marcin Mioduszewski is right - to this day it is not known what this Tunguska Unusual Thing really was. We are, in this particular matter, like blind men moving in the dark, who admittedly recognize some fragments of their surroundings, but the whole is unguessed. Such a condition was best expressed by the oft-cited Stanisław Lem, who wrote in "The Chain of Chance":

It's a puzzle in which each element individually is clear and transparent, but put together with others creates an unclear whole...

That's exactly right! Here Marcin Mioduszewski preaches a view that puts the virtue of moderation on a pedestal, and points out what astray we can be led by excessive enchantment with the New and the Unknown. For a young ufologist with a lot of experience, this attitude is a commendable example that not all young people in this country are drug addicts and madmen. This sober and realistic - despite the fantastic nature of the hypothesis linking TP to ETI - approach to the matter may in the future result in the solution of this intriguing mystery.

***

And now the last voice - a particularly valuable voice, because it comes from a specialist meteoritologist, and therefore the most knowledgeable person. In his speech, Andrzej Kotowiecki, M.A., develops his hypothesis, which is similar to the theory contained in pt. A-14 OF THE CANON..., and therefore the designation A-14a should be adopted for it, and he writes as follows:

14. A. Kotowiecki - TUNGUSKA EVENT VS. TECTITES?

Many dissertations and works have already been written about the event of June 30, 1908, in the area of the Podkamennaya Tunguska River, but this topic and this mystery still bothers many, including me.

What do we know about this event? What are the cold facts? I show what happened there in a telegraphic summary:

On the morning of June 30, 1908, residents of central Siberia in the Podkamennaya Tunguska River region noticed a fiery cloud stretching across the sky, which disappeared behind the horizon into the taiga.

At 07:17.11 local time, a terrifying explosion occurred.

Seismographs around the world recorded a terrible tremor, the epicenter of which was located NW of Lake Baikal.

The seismic wave was recorded in Washington.

At least 1,500 reindeer were killed in one of the villages in the Podkamennaya Tunguska region.

Passengers on a train traveling on the Trans-Siberian Iron Railway observed a glowing ball in the sky as big as the Sun, moving from south to north. The explosion was so huge, (600 kilometers from the epicenter), that the train's manager ordered the train to stop to check for damage.

Seismic stations in Tiflis (Tblisi), Tashkent and Jena registered the earthquake. In Irkutsk (900 kilometers from the epicenter), it took an hour before the pendulums of the seismographs calmed down.

People from the Evenk tribe reported: We were more than 80 km from the Tunguska River and saw the fire. The heat was so terrible that we had to lie down on the ground. "I was afraid," one of the Evenks later recounted, "that my shirt would catch fire on me".

A violent hurricane blew through the taiga.

The Angara River surged with a gigantic wave that swept away the rafters floating on the river so that only some of them were saved.

The airwave was recorded in St. Petersburg, Copenhagen and Washington, D.C., and the next day, with a 30-hour delay, it was recorded in Potsdam and London.

The day after the eruption, it was so bright in Bordeaux, France, that as late as 21:56 CEST it was still easy to read at a distance of 30 centimeters, while a day later at 21:15 a.m. a number of meteorological observatories noted a huge number of silvery clouds in the sky.

In 1968, Prof. N. Vasiliev calculated that the total area of these clouds must have been 10 million square kilometers.

In California, an actinometric station registered a strong opacity of the atmosphere and a significant reduction in solar radiation over the next three months.

Scientists realized that a powerful phenomenon had occurred in Siberia, but the first expedition did not get there until 20 years later. The expedition was led by L. Kulik, who in February 1928, from the top of Shakhorn, saw for the first time a gigantic area of completely destroyed taiga.

What happened in Siberia in a place at N 60°55' and E 101°57'?

What scientists noticed in 1928 and 1929/30 during the Kulik expedition?

No crater was found.

The total area of the destroyed taiga was almost 2,200 km2, with the taiga not broken at the epicenter.

It was calculated that the effect of such destruction could have given a nuclear bomb explosion of 20-40 Mt TNT at an altitude of 10-15 km. This exceeds 1-2 thousand times the power of the first atomic bomb.

Elevated radioactivity persisted for a long time in the disaster area, as evidenced by tree growth rings and measurements.

As late as 1961, scientists noticed traces on the branches of larches resembling burns from ionizing radiation.

It was not until 1964-68 that J. Lvov of the University of Tomsk discovered microscopic glass pellets measuring 0.02 - 0.15 mm. They were studied, among others, in the USA. According to the analysis of the Institute of Geology and Geography of the AN USSR, it was found that the silicates found in the balls are not found cither in the Earth's natural soils, industrial products or space objects. Gases such as hydrogen - H_2, hydrogen sulfide - H_2S and carbon dioxide - CO_2 were found inside the pellets.

These pellets are similar to small tektites!!! And this ties in with my theory about their origin, which I first presented in my paper, published in 1999, titled "Glaze not from Earth", and further developed in the paper "Tektites - Relics of Star Wars" presented, among others, on December 10, 2000 on "Nautilius Radia Zet". Therefore - in my opinion - it was not a meteorite, a cometary fragment, or a collision with Earth of antimatter. Descriptions of the crash tell me that it was undoubtedly a spacecraft (of the vimana type or similar design), built of glass and quartz, equipped with a nuclear reactor. At the same time, it may also have been part of a disintegrating, mysterious object called the BLACK PRINCE or BLACK BARON, whose disintegration was noticed by Soviet and American astronomers on December 18, 1955. At that time, the object broke up into 10 large debris, about 70 x 35 m in size, in orbit 2000. The process may have begun long before then.

The pellets found at the crash site are small in size, as, in my opinion, the explosion occurred in the Earth's atmosphere. The power of the energy was amplified by this, and with the presence of oxygen, a high temperature was generated. The ship simply evaporated, forming silvery clouds.

To date, tektites weighing several hundred kilograms have not been found. Mostly they weigh from a few to a few tens of grams - occasionally over 1 kg. According to my theory, it's as if a car windshield had disintegrated into a fine poppy in space, outside the Earth's atmosphere, and its pieces when flying through it took the shape of glass meteorites. Anyway, these large tektites are layered tektites called Muong Nong. They cooled down in layers.

In my opinion, they are an example of tektites that formed on Earth, near the cooling atomic stack.

Space vehicles made of materials such as glass or quartz can simultaneously constitute, as a whole, a "living computer organism" - i.e. a single integrated circuit very easy to operate. Confirmation of my theory about the origin of tektites is provided by the different-aged tektites found in the Zhamanshin impact crater in Kazakhstan, counting respectively: 0.7; 1.2 and 5.2 million years old - while the crater was formed z a l e d 10,000 years ago! It's as if a space vehicle built 5.2 million years ago was upgraded twice 1.2 and 0.7 million years ago, only to finally crash 10,000 years ago. As I have written many times before, a book based on a manuscript titled "Vaimanika Sastra," found in 1918 in the Barada Royal Sanskrit Library in Mysore, was published in India in 1973. This manuscript describes flying apparatuses of the vimana, rukma, sumdra and shokuna types. Among the most important verses I would include an explanation of the construction of the vimana, for which 27 different types of glass must be used(!!!). According to the description there, glass was used to build these small flying objects according to the following rules: 12 purified ingredients should be mixed according to the ratio of $5 : 3 : 5 : 1 : 10 : 10 : 11: 8 : 7 : 2 : 6 : 1$, put them in a lotus-shaped melting furnace and heated with charcoal. It should be heated to a temperature of 323 degrees [...]. The result will be shitaranjikaadarsa - that is, glass containing coolness. It is conjectured that this glass, like tektites, practically contained no water, that is, it was cool - dry, and at the same time could stay for a long time in space, where the temperature is close to Absolute Zero. At the same time, this text is evidence in support of the hypothesis of the origin of tektites. To sum up - I believe that tektites are parts and debris of space vehicles, built millions of years ago by gods and humans.

Of course, the crash of the object occurred in the atmosphere, low above the Earth, about 10-15 km, so we are not dealing here with specific tektites, but only small artifacts in the form of glass pellets. It seems to me that there may be more artifacts, but given the swampy terrain, as well as the fact that they didn't necessarily have to have fallen in this place, but to have gone many hundreds of kilometers away, it will be difficult to find them after so many years. And even if they were found, they will not be linked to the Tunguska Event.

Cieszyn, 2001-07-21

***

Hm... - that's a very bold hypothesis and boldly placed. But it explains at least a few phenomena unrelated to TP. I admit that the mystery of the tektites is still unsolved, but this one and only solution goes in the direction of starships and disasters - or even star wars... - and it is the original Polish theory on the subject.

Will this work bring us closer to solving the TCB puzzle? Us, perhaps not, but perhaps through the Internet it will reach someone who, in a flash of genius, Divine inspiration and intuition, will combine the facts known to us in such a way as to obtain the one and only true picture of what happened over the Tunguska taiga on the last day of June 1908...

In conclusion, I would like to thank very sincerely all those who helped me in the preparation of this book and referred to it critically and kindly. I hope that this work - although modest - will not be in vain and will be another milestone in our journey into the Unknown.

Jordanów, 2001-07-27, 08:09 CEST

15. R. Leśniakiewicz - TCB and visitors from outside the Solar System

Yet the picture would not be complete if it were not for recent discoveries of objects originating outside our Solar System. The last five years have brought us discoveries that shed new light on the TCB problem. Namely, that objects from other planetary systems have been discovered that have wandered into the vicinity of the Sun and planetary system.

15.1. Visitors from Space: meteorites

From time to time they fall to Earth and arouse great interest - not only among researchers. A nice or rare meteorite on the mineral and fossil market costs several thousand euros or dollars. But there is another reason to look for meteorites even at the bottom of the World ocean - it is their origin.

Prof. Dr. Avi Loeb wants to search for alien civilizations at the bottom of the ocean. This is not a foolish idea.

In October 2017, astronomers for the first time ever discovered an object in the Solar System that flew into our vicinity from another planetary system. This interstellar traveler, named

1I/'Oumuamua, had already flown out of the Solar System at the time, and there was no more opportunity to reach it and take samples. However, there must be more such objects. Prof. Avi Loeb of Harvard University has an idea for searching for them. A quite original one.

At the time of the discovery of 'Oumuamua, the object was "only" 30 million kilometers from Earth. The trajectory of its flight indicated that it could have come to us from the vicinity of Vega, the brightest star in the constellation of Lute. If this was indeed the case, the 25 light years separating Vega and the Sun could have been covered by the object in the last 300,000 years.

After flying past the point closest to the Sun in September 2017, the object began its journey outside the Solar System. Although its speed was decreasing, scientists noticed that it was not falling the way it should, quite as if it had its own energy source. The non-gravitational acceleration of the asteroid 'Oumuamua caused some scientists - including Prof. Avi Loeb - to suspect whether the inconspicuous asteroid was not some kind of artifact sent into space by representatives of an alien civilization. This idea at first glance seems crazy and completely frivolous. However, it is enough to think for a moment to realize that it is not unrealistic, after all, we ourselves are a civilization that in the last fifty years has sent space probes into interstellar space, which will also traverse space for billions of years and perhaps one day fly into some planetary system by accident. Such probes include Pioneer 10 and 11, Voyager 1 and 2, and finally the New Horizons probe. Since we could have sent such probes, so could some other civilization.

Since the discovery of 'Oumuamua, scientists have discovered one more interstellar object - comet 2I/Borisov, and recently also discovered one more object of this type in archival data.

On January 8, 2014, a meteoroid (later designated CNEOS-2014-01-08) entered Earth's atmosphere and its speed indicates that it came from outside the Solar System. Estimates indicate that this object entering the Earth's atmosphere was about a meter in diameter and had a mass of about 500 kg. It is also possible that part of the object survived its flight through the atmosphere and fell into the ocean.

15.2. Expedition for interstellar fish

Avi Loeb estimates that for every object the size of an 'Oumuamua (several hundred meters in diameter) in the Solar System, there could be a million objects like this meteoroid from 2014. Some of such objects may fall into the Earth's atmosphere. Some of them, in turn, may survive flight through the atmosphere and land on land or in the oceans. An object recorded in 2014 landed on the ocean floor near Papua New Guinea.

The scientist then poses the question, should we look into preparing a mission to catch up with 'Oumuamua, study its nature and bring back ground samples to Earth, or would it be better to prepare an expedition that would search for the remains of an interstellar meteorite on the ocean floor? The former mission would cost about a billion dollars, the latter about ten thousand times less.

Where CNEOS-2014-01-8 landed, the ocean is several kilometers deep, and the uncertainty of the landing site is about 10 kilometers. Certainly, the search for the remains will not be one of the easy ones, but theoretically it would be possible to locate the object with a powerful magnet, extract it from the ocean floor and transport it to laboratories on land. For the first time in history, humanity would have the opportunity to touch - literally - a rock from a planetary system other than the solar system. In the process, it would be possible to check whether it was definitely just a rock, or perhaps a product of alien technology, a sort of Voyager from another star.

Currently, a team working under the leadership of Professor Loeb at Harvard is engaged in preparing the design of such an exploration mission. Given Prof. Loeb's persistence and determination, we can expect that soon there will be some kind of research unit in the vicinity of Papua New Guinea, searching for an interstellar voyager at the bottom of the ocean.

And another interesting fact related to meteorites and the World ocean.

15.3. Asteroid fell into the Arctic Ocean - 2 hours after discovery!

Impact craters, meteorite discoveries, etc. The Tunguska explosion... We are witnessing our land being bombarded by space projectiles. It is said: time and again, asteroids approach or strike the Earth. While larger objects are under astronomical observation and their orbits are usually well known, this is not the case for smaller objects. They are so faint that they are often detected late or not at all. The problem is one 100-meter asteroid that has already been ignored - but fortunately missed.

15.4. Small and fast luminous spot

This is such a rare event, because on March 11, 2022, astronomers detected a chunk at least two meters in size just before impact. According to NASA and the European Space Agency (ESA), this is the fifth asteroid ever "caught" before re-entering the atmosphere and the first impactor (an object that hits the Earth) discovered by a European astronomer.

It is a discovery made by Krisztián Sárneczky of the Piszkéstető Observatory in Hungary, when he searched the sky with a 60-centimeter telescope in the evening hours of that day. At 20:24 CET, he spotted a small, fast-moving luminous spot. He took four consecutive pictures of the object and it became clear that it was a fast and close object - a NEO - a near-Earth object.

15.5. An alert has been issued

About 14 minutes later, the astronomer notified NASA Minor Planet Center of the sighting of the new object, which notified astronomers and other observatories. At the same time, NASA's special risk calculation system Scout calculated the trajectory of the object provisionally named 2022 EB5 based on the data it had. Scout initially had only data from 14 observations covering 40 minutes and identified the object as an impactor, explains David Farnocchia of NASA's Jet Propulsion Laboratory-JPL.

Just an hour after the discovery of the object, estimated to be two meters in size, ESA's Near-Earth Object Coordination Center (NEOCC) and NASA's Planetary Defense Coordination Office were alerted in an automated series of alerts. At that point, calculations had already predicted that the asteroid would hit the Arctic Ocean just an hour later, between 22:21 and 22:25 UTC.

15.6. Fall into the Arctic Ocean

And here's how it happened: at 22:22 UTC, the asteroid entered Earth's atmosphere about 140 km north of Jan Mayen Island - a little less than two hours after it was discovered. The fall was not observed in this desolate area. But a global network of ultrasonic sensors recorded the shock wave. The emitted energy of the impact was the equivalent of a M4.0 strong earthquake. Astronomers estimate that the Earth collides with such space objects 10 times a year - but such asteroids are discovered post factum... after the collision.

"Such small space bodies as 2022 EB5 fall into Earth's atmosphere quite often", said Paul Chodas, director of NASA's Center for Near-Earth Object Studies - CNEOS. "But because they are so small, they are very rarely detected in space hours before they fall. And on top of that, the right part of the sky should be visible to an observation telescope at the right time."

15.7. New telescopes for better observations

After all, asteroids, which are much larger and can cause serious damage, are usually discovered earlier. However, astronomers are working to further improve NEO observations. The Flyeye telescope, currently located at Monte Mufara, should contribute to this in the future In Italy Building. Its optics work in a similar way to the compound eyes of an insect, generating images from 16 partial exposures. (NB, the latest JWST - the James Webb Space Telescope works similarly.)

"The extremely wide field of view of these new telescopes will allow us to survey large areas of the sky in just one night, explains Detlev Koschny, head of the Planetary Defense Department at the European Space Agency. "Reduces the risk of losing a potentially important object.".

15.8. Comments

Why do I think Dr. Loeb's idea is right? It should be obvious. Our planet's World ocean covers almost ¾ of the Earth, so the majority of all meteorites that fall to Earth fall right into its waters. Meteorites occasionally hit Earth's floating vessels, causing damage to them. The search for cosmic "guests" at the bottom of the World ocean makes a lot of sense - if we find them somewhere, it's only there. Who knows if the mystery 1I/'Oumuamua is such a deserted robotic Bracewell probe that flew through the solar system, collected data and flew on?

A few years ago, for my part, I suggested penetrating any mine dumps in search of fossil meteorites. After all, in distant geological epochs they certainly fell to Earth more often and lingered as useless in mineral deposits - and today they are mined and no one takes care of them. And it's a pity, because among them there is probably more than one "guest from the stars".

And one more interesting fact. It was brought to my attention by the famous Kazimierz Bzowski, writing to me about the Greenland Meteorite, which fell to Earth on December 7 or 9, 1997 in Greenland. There would be nothing strange about this, if it were not for the fact that the energy of this impact was about 20-25 kt TNT - slightly more than the energy of the Little Boy atomic bomb explosion that turned Hiroshima into dust. The most interesting thing, however, is that this information was taken off the PAP world news service within 2 hours! - so that it was only reported by our "Super Express" with the pen of editor Ewa Jabłońska. Later, an article appeared in a magazine about the search for this very meteorite in Greenland, but which - supposedly - was not found. It's strange, but there should have been some trace of the impact left on the ice armor of Greenland - however, there was none, ergo either the meteorite exploded in the air, like TCB, or it wasn't a meteorite at all, or it was some military satellite of the Russians, Americans or Chinese, or maybe Atlanteans?... so far it's an "X-Files" case and there is no solution in sight.

Mr. Roman Rzepka is of the opinion that on December 9, 1997, a meteorite fell on Greenland in the vicinity of Nuuk (Godthåb), at N 64°20' - W 054°30', which moved at an extraordinary speed in the atmosphere of the Earth - as much as 56 km/s. so it appears that this meteorite came from the depths of the Galaxy! The remains of the meteorite were not found - reportedly... and this was the "pro" argument for orthodox scientists, claiming that such meteorites simply do not exist... - because they have no right to penetrate deep into the Solar System. A scientist who worked at the renowned Niels Bohr Institute in Copenhagen - Dr. Lars Lindberg Christiansen for expressing the view that this was an out-of-system meteorite, was simply fired from his job immediately... I myself remember a discussion in memorable July 1994 with a certain luminary of astronomy, who claimed that out-of-system meteorites are a pipe dream, just as the idea of the flow of matter between planetary systems of neighboring stars is nonsense. Luckily, just then Jupiter's atmosphere was panting hit by debris from comet D/1993 F2 or S-L 9!

So far, the Greenland Meteorite case is open. I suspect that it has been found, however, and has shared the fate of all inconvenient orthodox science artifacts like the "Gurtel cube" or the "Żabno sphere" - has been destroyed or is withering somewhere at the bottom of the basement of the Niels Bohr Institute or some American air base...

Another issue - the speed of flight of meteorites. Those 40-45 km/s with which these objects moved is not at all that astonishing. There are many meteorite swarms that move with v = 45-71 km/s, only that this is the speed of movement relative to the Earth, and in the cases described it is not so much about their speeds, but about trajectories. These objects move not in elliptical - closed orbits, but in hyperbolic - open trajectories. And this is the criterion.

So here we have something - not something to look for. And the search is worth it!

15.9. The mysterious IM1 object: a visitor from the Universe?

For some time I have been following the scientific press and websites, where from time to time scrolls information about a mysterious object, a meteorite rumored to have fallen near New Guinea not so long ago. "The Space Academy" writes about the out-of-system object No. 2 this way:

15.10. Second visitor from Space

A second interstellar visitor has arrived in the Solar System - and this time astronomers know where it came from.

When in 2017 A/2017 U1 - 1I/'Oumuamua flew through the Solar System no one knew where it came from. On the other hand, astronomers think they know where comet C/2019 Q4 Borisov - 2I/Borisov came from. Astronomers have found an object from outside the Solar System that flew by for the second time in history. But scientists think they have figured out where it came from this time.

The interstellar comet was first spotted by Gennady Borisov, an amateur astronomer in Crimea who was using his own telescope to observe the sky. When he found it, the object was the first interstellar visitor found since 2017, when the long 'Oumuamua passed by our solar neighborhood. In the publication, a group of Polish astronomers discovered how this new comet, called Comet 2I/Borisov or (in earlier descriptions) C/2019 Q4, got into the gravitational well of our Sun. And that path leads back to Kruger 60, which is a system of two red dwarfs 13.15 light years away.

Scientists have found that comet Borisov passed just 5.7 light years (ly) from the center of Kruger 60, 1 million years ago. This means that it was moving at a speed of just 2.13 mps (3.43 km/s).

From a human point of view, that's speed - about as fast as the X-43A Scramjet, which is one of the fastest aircraft ever created. But because of the Sun's gravity, the X-43A Scramjet can't leave our Solar System. And scientists discovered that if the comet was moving so slowly and was no more than 6 light-years away from Kruger 60, it wasn't just passing through. They thought it most likely came from that star system. Comet Borisov orbited these stars in the same way that comets in our system orbit our.

15.11 So the Kruger 60?

Ye Quanzhi, an astronomer and comet expert from the University of Maryland, who was not part of the project, has told "Live Science" that the evidence linking comet 2I/Borisov to Kruger 60 is very strong based on what we know so far.

"If you have a comet from another star system and want to find out where it came from, you need to check two things," he said. "First, was this comet close to a planetary system? Because if it's coming from there, its trajectory must pass through the location of that system.

Although the distance between the new comet and Kruger, at 5.7 ly, seems larger than a "small gap" (it is more than 357,000 times the distance between the Earth and the Sun - AU), it is close enough to be considered "small" for this kind of calculation," he said.

"Secondly," continued Ye, "comets are usually ejected from a planetary system when their gravity interacts with the major planets of that system."

In our solar system, this could look like Jupiter catching a falling comet, sending it into a short, partial orbit, and then ejecting it into the space between stars.

"This ejection velocity can be so high," said Ye. "It can't be infinite because planets have a certain mass," and how hard a planet can throw a comet into the void depends on its mass. He also said: "Jupiter is quite big, but you can't have a planet 100 times bigger than Jupiter, because then it would be a star."

Ye says this mass threshold limits the speed at which comets can move through the space between stars. And if their estimates of the comet's trajectory are correct, the authors of this study have shown that comet 2I/Borisov flew close enough to Kruger 60 in terms of speed and distance to suggest that it originated there.

Ye said: "Studying interstellar comets is exciting because it gives us a rare chance to study other solar systems with the same tools we use to study our own."

Astronomers can look at comet 2I/Borisov through telescopes that can give them information about the comet's surface. They can find out if it behaves like comets in our solar system (so far), or if it does something unusual, like 'Oumuamua. That's a whole area of research that's not normally possible for distant solar systems, where small objects appear only - if at all - as faint, discolored shadows on their suns.

With this research, everything we learn about comet Borisov could teach us something about Kruger 60, a nearby star system where no exoplanets have yet been found. On the other hand, 'Oumuamua appears to have come from the direction of the bright star Vega (α Lute), but astronomers at NASA's Jet Propulsion Laboratory believe it came from a new star system, although they don't know from which one. If these results are true, Comet Borisov will be the first object from another star system that has been traced back to its parent system.

But the people who conducted the study were cautious, saying that these results are not yet proof. Astronomers are still gathering information about the trajectory of Comet 2I/Borisov in space. More information may show that the original trajectory was wrong and that the comet came from somewhere else.

The article, which attempts to find out where the comet came from, has not yet been reviewed by other scientists, but is available on the arXiv preprint server.

That would be enough for now regarding the second out-of-system object. And yet, it turned out that there is a third and a fourth - and within our reach! The object in question is a meteorite designated as IM1[147], which fell into the Pacific Ocean a few years ago. And here is this footage of Aleksander Kowal:

IM1 hit the surface of the Pacific Ocean, in order to study it, the expedition must plunge to a depth of 1.7 kilometers.

According to a Harvard University researcher, in the waters of the Pacific Ocean, at a depth of less than two kilometers, may lie the remains of a ship belonging to an alien civilization.

Avi Loeb is a figure as prominent as controversial. For, on the one hand, he cannot be denied his scientific achievements, but on the other hand, it is not difficult to get the impression that his penchant for staying in the limelight - for a representative of the scientific world - is surprisingly high. Nevertheless, the information gathered so far suggests that something may indeed be afoot.

This is not the first time Loeb has spoken out about extraterrestrial life and its potential presence in the Solar System. If you remember the story of the mysterious interstellar object known as 'Oumuamua, it is worth noting that the Harvard University representative was one of the promoters of the theory that the extrasolar visitor was in fact a probe sent by aliens. This was to be indicated, among other things, by the unusual shape of the object and the way it moved.

---

[147] In the original 1M1.

Three years earlier there had been even closer contact, as a mysterious meteorite exploded over the Pacific Ocean on January 9, 2014. Named IM1, it became the focus of Loeb's attention, who decided to launch the Galileo project in 2021. It includes efforts to capture UFOs in high resolution.

The alleged alien craft was said to have plunged into the waters of the Pacific Ocean in January 2014.

Now, however, a scientist is trying to understand where IM1 came from and what it was in the first place. The object hit the surface of the Pacific Ocean at a gigantic speed and appeared harder than all the other meteorites described within the Center for Near Earth Object Studies catalog run by NASA. But how true can claims that IM1 was in fact a probe launched billions of years ago by an advanced alien civilization be?

With the approximate location where the mysterious object fell into the waters of the Pacific Ocean, researchers know where they should begin their search. The planned expedition could cost as much as $1.5 million and is to be launched from the Papua New Guinea area. The estimated depth where the remains of the extraterrestrial visitor could rest is up to 1.7 kilometers.

One of the latest breakthroughs in the ongoing project was the finding of peculiar spherules. Such small-sized spherules can be formed precisely due to meteorite impacts. Their violent explosions lead to such a scenario, and of particular interest in this case is the fact that the spherules from the Pacific Ocean have a very unusual composition. What is so astonishing about it? The main thing is the absence of nickel. Iron, magnesium and titanium were tracked instead. More detailed analyses will be needed to reach a final verdict on the matter. These are to use the mass spectrometry technique, by means of which it should be possible to identify the spherule's components with almost 100 percent certainty.

15.12. My 2 cents

A fourth extrasolar object is rumored to have fallen near Portugal, and perhaps it too will be retrieved. Of course, let's hope it doesn't end in some kind of disaster, as it did with the ill-fated DSV Titan...

The other day I threw out a suggestion to look for meteorites in mine dumps, I bet you'd find more than one, and an off-board one at that. It could be the same with spherulites - there could be a lot of them in the mine material! I do not know if anyone has taken an interest in this... Knowing the Poles, it is no one, because, after all, our "scientists" need to put everything under their noses, but who wants to rummage through heaps? If such a systematic search was carried out all over the world, such "visitors" from outer space would be found many, many more!

Were they alien spaceships? - Probably not, and even if they were, they could have been some Bracewell probes. Sending reconnaissance automatons into space makes more sense than living representatives of civilizations. Living beings are unique, while robots can be produced in any number. And this is the advantage of automated astronautics over regular astronautics. Until we find a way to cross space with "impunity", we will send robots - because it is both safer and cheaper. And the economic calculus applies both on Earth and in the farthest galaxy...

And another mystery of the Moon.

15.13. A radio-asteroid or nuclear device on the Moon?

Recent discoveries on the Moon are of understandable interest to science people and various fantasists (like me) and seekers of intelligent extraterrestrial life. Well, because the discovery of such a hot spot as the area between Compton and Belkovich craters is a sensation. This is what Kenneth Chang wrote about it in the pages of the New York Times a few days ago. And here is his article:

15.14. Scientists have discovered a hot spot on the other side of the Moon

Data from two Chinese orbiters have helped a team of scientists explain why a patch of lunar terrain is much warmer than the surrounding area.

Rocks beneath an ancient volcano on the far side of the moon remain surprisingly warm, scientists have revealed based on data from an orbiting Chinese spacecraft.

They point to a large slab of granite that solidified from magma in a geological drainage beneath the so-called Compton-Belkovich volcanic complex.

"I'd say we're hammering the nail in the coffin that this really is a volcanic feature," said Matthew Siegler, a scientist at the Planetary Science Institute based in Tucson, Arizona, who led the study. "But the interesting thing is that it's a very Earth-like volcanic feature."

The findings, which were published last week in the journal Nature, help explain what happened long ago under the strange part of the moon. The study also underscores the scientific potential of the data collected by China's space program, and how scientists in the United States have to get around obstacles to use the data.

For this study, Dr. Siegler and his colleagues analyzed data from microwave instruments on Chang'e-1, launched in 2007, and Chang'e-2, launched in 2010, two early Chinese spacecraft that are no longer operational. Because Congress currently prohibits direct cooperation between NASA and China, and the research was funded by a NASA grant, Dr. Siegler could not work with the scientists and engineers who collected the data.

"It was a limitation that we couldn't just call the engineers who built the instrument in China and say: 'Hey, how should we interpret this data?'," he said. "It would have been really great if we had worked with Chinese scientists on this all the time. But we're not allowed to. But fortunately they have made some of their databases public."

He was able to take advantage of the expertise of a Chinese scientist, Jianqing Feng, who met Dr. Siegler at the conference. Dr. Feng was working on a lunar exploration project at the Chinese Academy of Sciences.

"I realized that combining lunar exploration data from different countries would deepen our understanding of the Moon's geology and make exciting discoveries," Dr. Feng said in an email. "That's why I quit my job in China, moved to the United States and joined the Planetary Science Institute."

Both Chinese orbiters had microwave instruments, common in many Earth-orbiting weather satellites, but rare in interplanetary spacecraft.

Data from Chang'e-1 and Chang'e-2 thus provided a different picture of the moon, measuring heat flow up to 15 feet below the surface - and proved ideal for studying the Compton-Belkovich singularity.

Visually, the region is not distinguished by anything special. (It doesn't even have its own name; the combined name comes from the two neighboring impact craters, Compton and Belkovich.) Nevertheless, the region has fascinated scientists for several decades.

In the late 1990s, David Lawrence, then a scientist at Los Alamos National Laboratory, was working on data collected by NASA's Lunar Prospector mission and noticed a bright spot of gamma rays shooting from the site on the unseen side of the Moon. The energy of the gamma rays, the highest-energy form of light, corresponded to thorium, a radioactive element.

"It was one of those weird spots that stood out like a sore thumb in terms of the abundance of thorium," said Dr. Lawrence, now a planetologist at the Johns Hopkins Applied Physics Laboratory in Maryland. "I'm a physicist. I'm not an expert in the geology of the Moon. But even as a physicist, I noticed that this stood out and said: "OK, this is something worthy of further research."

More revelations came after the Lunar Reconnaissance Orbiter probe arrived in 2009. Bradley L. Jolliff, a professor of Earth and planetary sciences at Washington University in St. Louis, led the team that examined these high-resolution Compton-Belkovich images.

What they saw "suspiciously resembled a caldera," said Dr. Jolliff, referring to the remains of the volcano's rim. "When you consider that these features are billions of years old, they are remarkably well preserved."

A more recent analysis by Katherine Shirley, now at Oxford University in England, estimated the volcano's age at 3.5 billion years.

Because the lunar soil acts as a good insulator, dampening temperature fluctuations between day and night, the microwave emissions largely reflect the heat flow from inside the moon. "You only have to go about two meters below the surface to stop seeing solar heat," said Dr. Siegler.

At Compton-Belkovich, the heat flow was as high as 180 milliwatts per square meter, about 20 times the average for the highlands on the other side of the moon. This measure corresponds to a temperature of -10°F/23.33°C about six feet (about 180 cm) below the surface, or about 90°F/32.22°C warmer than elsewhere.

"This one stood out because it was simply hot compared to any other place on the Moon," said Dr. Siegler.

To produce so much heat and thorium gamma rays, Dr. Siegler, Dr. Feng and other researchers concluded that the most likely source was granite, which contains radioactive elements such as thorium, and that there must be a lot of it.

"It seems to more accurately determine what kind of material is really underneath," said Dr. Lawrence, who was one of the reviewers of the paper for Nature.

"It's sort of the tip of the iceberg," he said of primordial gamma-ray emissions. "What you see at Compton-Belkovich is a kind of superficial expression of something much larger underneath."

Volcanism is visible elsewhere on the moon. Plains of hardened lava - lakes or seas of basalt - cover vast stretches of the surface, mostly on the nearer side. But Compton-Belkovich is different, resembling some volcanoes on Earth, such as Mount Fuji and Mount St. Helens, which spit out more viscous lava.

A small part of the Compton-Belkovich volcanic complex. The upper two-thirds of the scene shows the volcanic complex; the lower third of the image is outside the complex.

It appears that granite is rare in other parts of the solar system. On Earth, granite is formed in volcanic regions where oceanic crust is pushed beneath the continent by plate tectonics, geological forces that push pieces of the Earth's outer crust. Water is also a key component of granite.

But the Moon is mostly dry and lacks plate tectonics. Moon rocks brought back by NASA astronauts more than 50 years ago contained only a few grains of granite. But data from Chinese orbiters suggest a granite formation more than 30 miles/48 km wide below Compton-Belkovich.

"Now we need geologists to figure out how to produce these kinds of features on the Moon without water, without plate tectonics," said Dr. Siegler.

Dr. Jolliff, who was not involved in the research, said the article was "a very nice new contribution." He said he hopes NASA or another space agency will send a spacecraft to Compton-Belkovich to conduct seismic and mineralogical measurements.

Such a mission could primarily help test ideas about how the volcano formed there. One hypothesis is that a plume of hot matter rose from the mantle beneath the crust, much like under the Hawaiian islands.

For Dr. Feng, his current visa authorizing him to work in the United States is about to expire. He is applying for a new one, navigating his research career amidst the geopolitical disputes between the US and China.

"We are now starting to study other potential granite systems on the Moon," he said. "In addition, we will expand our models to study the icy moons of Jupiter. That's why I'm trying to stay in the United States as long as possible."

Volcanic calderas (top) and impact craters (bottom) in the Compton-Belkovich area indicative of its volcanic origin.

15.15. Hot spot - a trackside mystery

Granites on the Moon, a "hot spot" - and why not? This would be tangible evidence of lunar volcanism. After all, there are "hot spots" on the visible side of the Moon, which are located in the locations of such impact craters as Copernicus, Aristarchus, Aristillus and Kepler. Gas ejaculations from under the surface of the Silver Globe are taking place there - mainly carbon dioxide and argon.

Water vapor is emitted in several places, the most famous of which is the Rainier Gamma formation. What's more, the water that escapes there is apparently salty as in Earth's oceans. Something like this occurs on the moons of Jupiter, Saturn and Uranus.

Yet I don't think these are manifestations of volcanic activity. There is a possibility that these are gases deposited beneath the moon's surface ejected by thermal expansion. During the lunar night, the temperature drops, the gas stops escaping and such activity ceases.

One more possibility, namely - a long, long time ago - some 3.2 billion years ago a radio asteroid crashed into the Moon. Part of it scattered around the area creating a radioactive stain of its debris, while the other part stuck into the ground and radiated... NB, the age of such a radioasteroid could tell us more than a little about the origin and early history of the Universe or Miltiuniversum. After all, something like this could be a visitor from another star system, another galaxy or even another Universe!

So much for natural causes. As for the unnatural ones, it is obviously the activity of some rational beings who had on the Moon some kind of energy plant operating on the basis of much safer than uranium and plutonium - thorium 232 – ^{232}Th*, which only after T1/2 = 14 billion years decays to the isotope ^{228}Ra* and finally to ^{208}Pb thanks to which it is so safe. This would have to be thoroughly investigated - perhaps there would be some traces of aliens or beings from planet Earth... Of course, these could be other nuclear devices, but they would all be related to obtaining energy. Perhaps they were smashed during the impact of some asteroid or deliberately destroyed during the Atomic War of the Gods-Astronauts, which Dr. Miloš Jesenský wrote about at one time. But we will know this no sooner than after an expedition to that part of the Moon.

Jordanów, 2023-07-20

16. Sources:

Bzowski Kazimierz - "Sieć Wilka", Rybnik 1999

Desonie Danielle - "Kosmiczne katastrofy", Warsaw 1997

Eleonora - "Tajemnice kamiennych kręgów", Katowice 1998

Grobicki Aleksander - "Nie tylko Trójkąt Bermudzki", Gdańsk 1980

Jesenský Miloš - "Bohové atomových válek", Ústi nad Labem 1998

Kotowiecki Andrzej - "Szkliwo nie z tej Ziemi", Cieszyn 1999

Krzyściak Jan - "Däniken, Kosmici i Atlantydzi", Katowice 1997

Marks Andrzej - "W poszukiwaniu Kosmitów", Warsaw 1979

Marks Andrzej - "Pod znakiem komety", Warsaw 1986

Mora Aleksander - "Atomowe wojny bogów", Lublin 1979

Mostowicz Arnold - "My z Kosmosu", Warsaw 1977

Mostowicz Arnold - "O tych, co z Kosmosu", Warsaw 1987

Mostowicz Arnold - "Spór o synów nieba", Warsaw 1994

Niedzicki Wiktor - "Tajemnice Ziemi", Warsaw 1984

Pikulski Andrzej S. - "Nieziemskie skarby", Warsaw 1999

Rzepecki Bronisław, Piechota Krzysztof - "UFO nad Polską", Białystok 1997

Schneigert Zbigniew - "Broń i strategia nuklearna", Warsaw 1983

Schneigert Zbigniew - "Zagrożenie z Kosmosu", Warsaw 1984

Szałek Benon Zbigniew - "Korzenie Wyspy Wielkanocnej", Szczecin 1995

Tazieff Haroun - "Kratery w płomieniach", Warsaw 1958

Tazieff Haroun - "Woda i ogień", Warsaw 1953

Tollmann Alexander, Tollmann Edith - "A jednak był Potop", Warsaw 1999

Witkowski Igor - "Księga dowodów", Warsaw 1999

Yeomans Donald K. - "Komety", Warsaw 1999

Znicz-Sawicki Lucjan - "Goście z Kosmosu: Katastrofa Tunguska - Trójkąt Bermudzki - Obce ślady", Gdańsk 1982

Kieta Katarzyna - "UFO nad Alwernią" in the "Gazeta Krakowska" no. 119, 120, 127, 128, 129/1999

Mietelski Jan - "Co spada z nieba w Polsce" in the "Wiedza i Życie" no. 5/1993

Mioduszewski Marcin - "Czy NOO naprawdę latają nad Małopolską?" - paper for a meeting with readers on July 2, 1999 in Kraków, Internet: *www.ufocentrum.w.pl*

Płeszka Janusz, Ściężor Tomasz - "Zdarzenie w Jerzmanowicach w oczach miłośnika astronomii", Kraków 1993 - script

Płeszka Janusz, Ściężor Tomasz - "Analiza ruchu ciała meteorytowego w atmosferze", Kraków 1994 - script

Płeszka Janusz, Ściężor Tomasz - "Co zdarzyło się w Jerzmanowicach 14 stycznia 1993 roku?" in the "Urania" no. 6,1993

Soczówka Bartosz - "Przegląd obserwacji Nieznanych Obiektów Orbitalnych/Gwiazdopodobnych" - MCBUFOiZA report online at *www.ufocentrum.w.pl*

Szulc Anna - "Kosmiczne trzy po trzy" in the "Gazeta Krakowska" of October 1, 1994

Szulc Anna, Pieczara Izabella - "Wózek na krzywych kółkach" in the "Gazeta Krakowska" of January 28-29, 1995

Włodarczyk Krzysztof - "Meteoryt nad Jerzmanowicami" in the "Młody Technik" no. 5/1993

Włodarczyk Krzysztof - "Bolid nad Jerzmanowicami" in the "Postępy astronomii" no. 3,1994

Bernatowicz Robert - "Meteoryt Tunguski" in the "Nautilus Radia Zet" - a series of three programs on Radio Zet in 1998

Trojanowski Maciej - "Bolid Jerzmanowicki" - two programmes of the cycle "Nie do wiary", TVN, September 1999

Radek Kosarzycki - *https://www.msn.com/pl-pl/wiadomosci/nauka-i-technika/avi-loeb-chce-poszukiwa%C4%87-obcych-cywilizacji-na-dnie-oceanu-to-nie-jest-g%C5%82upi-pomys%C5%82/ar-AAWkhxc?ocid=winp1taskbar&cvid=2c4589e1531d4be08a741cbd17224f31&fbclid=IwAR0YIbHi5JgrUnbCpTPnLTDokr36S75zVdWYEdg4s93_EKLt9nLHNt9ODcs*

Abigail Anderson - *https://www.socialpost.news/an-asteroid-hit-the-arctic-ocean-just-two-hours-before-it-was-discovered/*

https://blog.thespaceacademy.org/2023/06/a-second-interstellar-visitor-has.html?fbclid=IwAR2JI6JvA_6fq3SBoLke9-x2lKmunYIgSQ1vUGEbnrnwIw8q3oDkxM3X92c

https://www.focus.pl/artykul/statek-obcych-szczatki-w-pacyfiku-1m1

https://www.nytimes.com/2023/07/11/science/moon-hot-spot-granite.html